Δ   The Triangle Papers: 63

MW01017121

The
Global Economic Crisis

A Report to
The Trilateral Commission

North American Author
E. GERALD CORRIGAN

European Author
SIR CALLUM MCCARTHY

Pacific Asian Author
NAOKI TANAKA

PAUL A. VOLCKER

BILL EMMOTT

Published by
The Trilateral Commission
Washington, Paris, Tokyo
2010

The Trilateral Commission was formed in 1973 by private citizens of Europe, Japan, and North America to foster closer cooperation among these three industrialized regions on common problems. It seeks to improve public understanding of such problems, to support proposals for handling them jointly, and to nurture habits and practices of working together. The Trilateral countries are nations in Europe, North America and Pacific Asia. They include the member and candidate member nations of the European Union, the three nations of North America, Japan, South Korea, the Philippines, Malaysia, Indonesia, Singapore, Thailand, Australia, New Zealand, China, and India.

These essays were prepared for the Trilateral Commission and are distributed under its auspices. They were discussed at the Commission's annual meeting in Dublin on May 8, 2010.

The authors—from North America, Europe, and Pacific Asia—have been free to present their own views. The opinions expressed are put forward in a personal capacity and do not purport to represent those of the Trilateral Commission or of any organization with which the authors are or were associated.

Library of Congress Cataloging-in-Publication Data

Corrigan, E. Gerald.
  The global economic crisis / E. Gerald Corrigan, Callum McCarthy, Naoki Tanaka.
    p. cm.
  ISBN 978-0-930503-93-2
  1. Global Financial Crisis, 2008-2009. 2. Financial services industry--Deregulation.
3. Money market. 4. Economic policy. 5. Capital movements. 6. Globalization--
Economic aspects. I. McCarthy, Callum. II. Tanaka, Naoki, 1945- III. Title.
  HB3722.C697 2010
  330.9--dc22
                    2010028967

The Trilateral Commission

www.trilateral.org

1156 15th Street, NW
Washington, DC 20005

5, rue de Téhéran
75008 Paris, France

Japan Center for International Exchange
4-9-17 Minami-Azabu
Minato-ku
Tokyo 106-0047, Japan

Contents

The Authors

North American Author

E. Gerald Corrigan is a managing director at Goldman Sachs. He is cochair of the Firmwide Risk Management Committee, vice chair of the Firmwide Business Practices Committee, a member of the Firmwide Commitments Committee, and chairman of the Goldman Sachs Bank USA. He joined the firm as a managing director in 1994 and was named partner in 1996. Jerry ended a twenty-five-year career with the Federal Reserve System when he stepped down from his position as president and chief executive officer of the Federal Reserve Bank of New York in 1993. He had been chief executive officer of the New York Fed and vice chairman of the Federal Open Market Committee since 1984. He has also served as president of the Federal Reserve Bank of Minneapolis and as special assistant to Federal Reserve chairman Paul A. Volcker.

European Author

Sir Callum McCarthy is the former chairman of the UK Financial Services Authority (FSA), where he served from 2003 to 2008. He is currently chairman of J. C. Flowers & Co UK Ltd; a nonexecutive director of the Industrial and Commercial Bank of China; a nonexecutive director of the U.S. company, IntercontinentalExchange; and a member of the board of HM Treasury. Before becoming chairman of the FSA, he was the chairman and chief executive of the UK energy regulator, Ofgem (1999–2003). He has worked as an investment banker in London, Tokyo, and New York.

Pacific Asian Author

Naoki Tanaka is president of the Center for International Public Policy Studies, Tokyo, and a freelance economic critic specializing in a variety of fields, including international and Japanese economics, politics, and industry. He graduated from the University of Tokyo Faculty of Law and finished all coursework for a Ph.D. at the Economic Research Division. He was previously president of the 21st Century Public Policy Institute, and has served as chairman of the Postal Privatization Committee, chairman of the Financial System Council since 1998, member of the Fiscal System Council since 2001, and vice chairman of the Fiscal System Council since 2009. His publications include *Money's Seizing Up* (2008), *What is Structural Reform* (2001), and *The Market and Government* (2000).

Paul A. Volcker served in the U.S. government for almost thirty years during five presidential administrations. Appointed as chairman of the Board of Governors of the Federal Reserve System by President Jimmy Carter in 1979, he was reappointed by President Ronald Reagan in 1983. After leaving the Federal Reserve in 1987, he became professor of international economic policy (now emeritus) at Princeton University and served as chairman of the firm of James D. Wolfensohn & Co. until his retirement in 1996. In 2004, he was called on to lead an independent investigation into the Iraqi Oil for Food Program of the United Nations and in 2007 to lead a review of the World Bank's anticorruption efforts. In 2008, President-elect Barack Obama chose Mr. Volcker to head the President's Economic Recovery Advisory Board. Mr. Volcker is chairman of the Board of Trustees of the Group of 30 (G30), an international organization that examines the impact of economic and financial decisions by the public and private sectors. As chairman of the first National Commission on the Public Service (the "Volcker Commission") in 1988 and the second Volcker Commission in 2002, he established himself as one of the nation's strongest advocates for the revitalization of the public service.

Bill Emmott was editor of *The Economist* from 1993 until March 31, 2006, when he stepped down in order to concentrate on writing books. He worked for *The Economist* for twenty-six years in all, as a correspondent in Brussels and Tokyo and as financial and business editors. While he was editor, the worldwide circulation more than doubled to 1.1 million copies a week. He is the author or coauthor of six books, four of which have been about Japan. He published *The Sun Also Sets* in English and Japanese in 1989 and *The Sun Also Rises* in 2006. His latest book, *Rivals: How the Power Struggle between China, India and Japan Will Shape Our Next Decade,* was published in 2008. Bill Emmott was a Trilateral Commission task force author on *Managing the International System over the Next Decade* (with Koji Watanabe and Paul Wolfowitz, 1997).

1

Paul A. Volcker and Bill Emmott
A Conversation

This is a transcription of a conversation between Paul A. Volcker and Bill Emmott as part of the program of the Trilateral Commission's plenary meeting in Dublin on May 8, 2010.

Bill Emmott: Good morning, ladies and gentlemen. We are here before you to discuss what is described as "the international financial situation," which some may describe as God's work and others may describe as the devil's work. But we have, fortunately, the Pope, Paul Volcker, in order to interpret this for us.

Paul needs no introduction, but I would point out, since we are going to discuss finance, financial innovation, and financial regulation, that he is on record as having said two things recently. One was that the last useful financial innovation that he could remember was the automated teller machine. The second thing that he said, I think, in a Senate hearing, was that he warned that there had better be better financial regulation by the time of the next financial crisis. He recognized that he might not be alive when it happened, but if it wasn't properly done he threatened to come back and haunt the ones who failed. Have I got that accurately, Paul?

Paul A. Volcker: More or less.

Emmott: More or less, exactly. But I'm a journalist, so one doesn't get them quite right.

We're going to start off by having a discussion, and then of course opening up to you for the important part, for questions. I think that given the situation in the debt markets yesterday, particularly in Europe, and the fact that none other than the prime minister of Italy—a man with whom I do not often agree—described the situation in the eurozone as being a "state of emergency" yesterday, we have, in the world economy, seen a replacement of excessive private debt with rescue-oriented public debt. Are we now, Paul, seeing a sovereign debt crisis unfolding before us, in your opinion?

In Europe, we spent a lot of our time pointing our fingers at Wall Street, saying that all the problems were coming from America.

Volcker: We're glad to share that burden of where the problems come from. I think this is obviously a great test of the euro, and therefore has wider significance for Europe. I look at this from a particular viewpoint of having thought the euro was a good idea. Ten or twenty years ago, there weren't many American economists who agreed with that view. The view that was often expressed was that you cannot bring a disparate group of countries together in a single currency, a single central bank, without a government overseeing it. It wouldn't hold together. Well, now we're going to see whether it's going to hold together.

I wish I could be as optimistic as Mario Monti was yesterday, in saying that the crisis will bring about a resolution that will make it all stronger. But I think what we're seeing here is contrary to what the hope was, which is that the common currency would force discipline on member countries. There was this stability pact, or whatever it was called, to force fiscal discipline on various countries. In fact, this does not work. The fact that all countries could benefit from a low interest rate and from a stable currency has kind of promoted excesses. That has taken place in other countries as well, but the common currency did not stop it.

Emmott: Let's say that Jean-Claude Trichet got on the telephone to you and said, "As a central banker, how should I respond to this crisis?" What would you be advising him as the European Central Bank?

Volcker: Well, he's already got interest rates pretty low, but you have some rules within Europe that I'm not an expert on as to what kind of credits he can take in providing credit in the normal course—or the abnormal course, under the circumstances—of the European Central Bank. The temptation, and I suppose what will happen in the end, is the loosening of some of those collateral requirements to help smooth over a crisis situation.

Emmott: I remember during the time when the Fed was constantly re-defining . . . .

Volcker: The Fed has done it on a great scale, so you would be in very good company.

Emmott: Absolutely. What will be the consequences for the Fed of having done that? I recall at the time it was doing that widening . . . you nodded your head in horror at that. So are we now going to see that in Europe too? Actions do not generally come consequence-free.

Volcker: When you look at the Federal Reserve, a lot of questions arise, not just over the reaction to the crisis, but why did the crisis come about? To what extent did monetary policy contribute to that, and, maybe more relevantly, to what extent did too-lax supervision contribute to it? I look at the central bank, the Federal Reserve, as the major banking regulator in the United States. They were not alone, but together I think it's fair to say that there was a failure in banking regulation. The Federal Reserve reacted with great force in terms of the crisis itself, but the relaxation of the old standards obviously raises other questions.

The Federal Reserve has lost its invulnerability, if it ever had any, but it's subject to political and other attacks. My sense is that it's going to emerge from this reexamination pretty well, considering the fact that there was a great antagonism toward the Federal Reserve a few months ago. There was some risk that all their regulatory authority would be taken away and that the structure of the system might be more impaired. That has not happened. They are going to retain a lot of regulatory authority, maybe even be reinforced as the primary banking supervisor. But it certainly has raised questions. It's going to be some time before it can reestablish a kind of unquestioned sense of regulatory authority in the United States as well as credibility in monetary policy.

Emmott: You can take from that cycle, as we say, a sense of reassurance for the European Central Bank, which worries a lot about losing its independence, about getting involved in politics, about treading into dangerous minefields. The Fed's experience is in a much less naturally independent setting.

Volcker: I've been looking at it from outside, obviously. It seems to me the European Central Bank has gained a lot of credibility in a difficult situation over the past ten years. Now that credibility will be tested under these circumstances. Can they relax some of the restrictions enough, in terms of the collateral requirements we were talking about and other things, and retain their essential credibility? My impression is they've built up enough credibility so that they can do that kind of thing and react flexibly, but it's obviously going to raise questions about, again, the relationship between the European Central Bank and the political management of Europe.

Emmott: Let's move on to the United States, first of all the economy, but then swiftly to the financial reform bill and all of that process. We saw very good jobs numbers yesterday, or at least—confusingly with these things—the job creation was terrific but unemployment still went up.

Volcker: I saw it briefly on television, but I can't say much about the economy that you don't already know. We're in a period of several quarters now of expanding economic activity. Some of these job numbers, and the most recent growth in industrial production, I'm sure are related heavily to the reversal of the inventory liquidation, which was very strong earlier, to no liquidation and maybe some accumulation. That provides quite a little push to industrial production at the moment, and some employment.

But I still think the outlook over a period of time is for what I like to think of as kind of a slog—an increase, but not very fast. Because some of the basic drivers of the economy, or what I'd like to see as some of the basic drivers of the economy—business investment and exports—I don't think are going to rise very fast since too much spending is constrained, or should be constrained. We can't build the economy on another consumer boom. Housing isn't going to go anyplace for a while, so I think sluggish growth is likely. Unemployment is going to remain high for a while.

Emmott: And the fiscal consolidation process. It's not there.

Volcker: That's a vision for the future, fiscal consolidation. But I don't think you're realistically going to consolidate the fiscal side in the midst of this high unemployment and this sluggish growth. And you shouldn't. I have no problem with that. The question is whether we'll do it in a timely fashion once the economy gets a little more momentum, and that's always a question.

It's a question for monetary policy too: how fast, and when, does monetary policy begin moving toward a less easy posture, a less accommodative posture? Those are always extremely difficult questions, and we'll see how they manage it this time. But it's well understood, and the Federal Reserve Board understands their challenge. I'm sure that President Obama is very aware of the fiscal challenge, but you can't do much about it now.

We have this commission, this fiscal commission, and you can approach that cynically. But I'm always in favor of the commission because it provides some kind of a forum to help educate the country on what will be necessary, even if they don't say "Here's an answer" and it gets enacted. That's very unlikely. But it can, I think, go some distance toward helping to lay the groundwork for a fiscal program maybe two years down the road.

Emmott: A striking thing for a layman about this crisis, which really started three years ago, is that it was all about lack of financial regulation, we thought. What has been done on either side of the Atlantic to change that? The answer is, very little, though a 1,300-page bill has landed in Congress. The first question on that is, Does it concern you that three years have passed without anything happening, or was that an appropriate response in that legislating in haste and in the middle of a crisis probably would have been a mistake?

Volcker: I think it probably is appropriate, in hindsight. At the time we thought everything should go faster. We know some of the answers. Let's get it done. But it's a very complicated situation, and sitting back a little bit and having a little chance at putting something together will be more coherent. You speak about the 1,300-page bill, which I was moaning about myself. But I had a look at the bill the other day—there isn't much on each page! It's big print, and short pages. But it's still too big and too cumbersome.

The underlying problem we have here, which we're not going to get a definitive answer to, is that this enormous edifice of financial engineering, and complicated finance, and the rise of derivatives and all that stuff, led to an immense generation of wealth in the financial community. But has this really stimulated any real growth in productivity or the economy? I'm a little bit of a cynic on this, and I find it a little difficult to detect that enormously favorable impact on the economy. The question is whether it's made the economy more vulnerable to crisis. The whole edifice of the argument was that we were going to diffuse and chop up the risk, and send it to people who were able to bear the risk, and all the rest. But the risk somehow seemed to get pretty concentrated in the end, and when it became unraveled, the complications of the market made it more difficult to deal with. Your attitude toward that affects what you want to do in regulation, and how far you want to take the regulation.

Adair Turner, the head of the British Financial Services Authority, has been very articulate on this subject, and I think a lot of the stuff that he's been writing deserves a lot of attention. He very broadly comes to the conclusion that there are pluses and minuses of the new financial system, but it can stand a little regulation, and don't be afraid to tinker with it and restrain it from its excesses. I think that's the correct answer.

Emmott: Yes, and we are starting to see studies coming out attempting to assess the cost of tighter financial regulation in terms of future economic growth. I wonder, How on earth do you calculate this?

Volcker: I think the burden of my argument is, Don't be afraid of a little regulation because these enormous benefits have not been all that clear, and arguably they've gotten us in trouble. I have to say, one of the saddest days of my life was when my brilliant oldest grandson told me he wanted to become a financial engineer. I wondered whether that was a career path that he would find satisfying over a period of time, or whether his grandfather would find it satisfying over a period of time. But I don't think we should be afraid of entering into the market in areas that we think need reform, and reform them.

Emmott: The test must be the cost and the ease of borrowing for end users, and whether that's appropriate, isn't it?

Volcker: The cost of borrowing for companies in the end is going to be determined by the interaction between monetary policy and economic activity. That has a powerful effect on interest rates and the cost of capital, and I don't think all this manipulation has much to do with it, frankly.

Emmott: What do you think is going to emerge from the sausage machine of Congress on the financial reform bill? How much of the Volcker rule will be there?

Volcker: I think we're going to get a better bill than we would have gotten a year ago. It isn't perfect. There are a lot of things in it I don't like, but there are a number of central points I think I do like.

There are several key points that are going to get a lot of debate. One is to what degree do you corral in derivatives? And, importantly, to what extent can you get them on organized exchanges and clearinghouses and so forth? There's a pretty good consensus on that. There's some effort to go much further, but I think that it will come out okay. I don't think the more extreme proposals for practically pushing the commercial banks entirely out of the derivatives business are going to end up as part of the legislation. That's an important area.

With this idea of resolution authority—the central problem of too big to fail and moral hazard—a lot of weight is being put upon the idea that some agency can step in, take a failing financial institution, take it over, have enough resources to manage it in the short run, but basically liquidate the organization. And this feeling that the big organizations are going to be saved, the managements will continue, the stockholders will survive, the creditors will be protected—the whole idea is, no, get this mechanism that can go in there and efficiently dispose of the failing institution. I like to think of it as a decent burial, but not on life support.

There's a little skepticism about this. Is it really possible? I understand the skepticism, particularly for big banks, which are central to the economy. I've helped introduce a wrinkle that says that these big banks ought to pay attention to the basic banking business because that is vital to the economy. They run the payment system, they make loans, they provide safe deposit facilities. In fact, they were protected during the crisis, so that kind of reinforced the idea of safe deposit facilities.

But they shouldn't be engaging in some of these more exotic speculative activities because there's an implication of public support. They are subject to the Federal Reserve—not just regulation but to Federal Reserve liquidity facilities. Their deposits are insured and they have an advantage in the markets. In fact, they have taxpayer support, and taxpayers ought to be supporting essential activities. They shouldn't be supporting speculative activities. The decision ought to be made to separate out the commercial banking business from the rest of the financial markets.

Will this new resolution authority be able to take care of the nonbanks when they get in trouble and fail, without bringing down the whole system? That's the theory behind this, and I think it's a reasonable theory. I hope it works, and elsewhere I think there is sort of a consensus around it in principle, particularly in Europe. But we've got to bring it together.

There's been some criticism of the United States moving without the rest of the world. I think the rest of the world would not move without somebody leading, and I hope the kind of recent momentum we have in the United States, and this reform effort, can be melded into and help inspire a more general agreement among at least the leading countries, the UK and continental Europe, and, for that matter, I think the Japanese and the Chinese will come along.

Emmott: This issue of separating out commercial banking, like a narrower definition, from the rest, there's not that much discussion of that in the UK, though some people have floated it, particularly in the *Financial Times*. But there's not been very much discussion of that at a serious level. Part of what's behind the lack of that discussion is the thought that if we make them disclose everything they're doing and then slap the appropriate capital leverage ratio rules on them, we can just let them get on with it. Why is that wrong in your view? Why not just do that?

Volcker: There's kind of an immediate consensus on a crisis, which is that the regulators have to get together, and they've got to review capital requirements, and they've got to review liquidity requirements, and they've got to review other things that they can do together and should do together to avoid regulatory arbitrage. And where do we do it? We have the organization for doing it and the tradition for doing it in Basel. That's fine. That process is going on, and I think it is important.

But I observe that there, two years after the crisis, there have been wonderful papers written about the problem and how to do it. But I am told—and I'm not close to this at all, but I think there's some reality to what I'm told—when it comes to specific decisions, they're having great difficulty because they've got twenty or thirty countries involved, all of which have a particular interest. It's an old story. So they find it very difficult to conclude upon just how to do those capital requirements, how to do those liquidity requirements, what leverage requirements are appropriate for different banks and different countries. It's hard getting a consensus. I hope and believe they will eventually get it. They've got very good leadership. But I think the problem of relying entirely upon regulatory and supervisory authority is to maintain discipline over a period of time without some kind of strong structural points written in the law that provide a focus for the regulators.

When things are going well it is very hard for any supervisory system to maintain real discipline. The unanswerable argument is, "What are you restraining us for, everything is going well?" And, "You're only interfering with God's work." That's a very difficult argument to deal with. A great statement is that the central banks take the punchbowl away just when the party's getting good, but deciding when the party's getting good is precisely what's difficult. When it's really getting good, nobody wants the punchbowl taken away, so can we develop some structural elements in the system that hopefully provide protection for the regulators so they can maintain discipline?

Emmott: One of the extraordinary things about this whole thing is how difficult it is to work out who's drunk in the party. The lack of knowledge, even now, of which banks have exposure to Greece— this is the government bond market and sovereign loans—and, really, we don't know.

Volcker: The market is much more international, much more complex. All those interrelationships are much harder to sort out than they were twenty years ago when I was involved.

Emmott: We'll open up for questions in a second, but, in terms of dealing with modern finance, two issues come up. One is, Are financial institutions simply too politically powerful? People have written of it being essentially a financial oligarchy, one of the Russian post-Soviet oligarchies. Do you think that's right, or do you feel sorry for Lloyd Blankfein?

Volcker: It's too strong, but there's no doubt that there's been a lot of money made in finance, and they have not been shy about using some of that money to grease the political wheels. There is, however, blowback about that now from the population in general. I think you see that very clearly in Congress, that some of this lobbying is not so effective when there's a feeling in the country that something's the matter in the world of finance and something's the matter with big banks. So I think the view that you express is a bit over the top.

Emmott: Yes. But in the United States, the politics of it has moved against the banks, quite strongly.

Volcker: I don't think it's unreasonable to put some limits on a bank's size. The Treasury has made a proposal that doesn't seem unreasonable to me, which really amounts to something like an American financial institution should not have more than 10 percent of the market. Given the size of the American market, that doesn't seem to me an undue limitation on the size of the organization, and not any limitation on their ability to compete internationally or otherwise. There's a degree of concentration in banking in the United States that is unbelievable compared to attitudes in the United States twenty years ago when we didn't even have banking across state lines.

Emmott: Indeed, very recently. Given the complexity of the system and the size of some of these institutions, and coming back to this issue of the Federal Reserve—in my country it will be the Bank of England, at least if the Conservative Party carry out their manifesto pledge—do you think central banks are capable of having responsibility for such a complex system?

Volcker: It's a challenge. But I think they're not only capable of it, they had better be involved, because the nature of their responsibilities and the nature of their contacts with the market lead, I think, to a complementarity between regulation and monetary policy. Not everybody agrees with that. They think it may be complex and it's better to keep them separate, and that's the way the Brits went more than ten years ago. There's some rethinking of that in Britain, and I think that's right. There ought to be some rethinking. I don't think the Federal Reserve or any central bank has to be dominant or a total regulator. But if you insulate them from the market and you take away all their regulatory responsibilities, my sense is that you're going to get worse monetary policy, not better.

Emmott: But will you get better banking supervision? That's the key question.

Volcker: Yes, I think the corollary is better banking supervision. There's a tendency for a banking regulator to be a little bit myopic, especially if that's their only responsibility. When things are going well, they don't want to interfere, as I said. When things are going badly and they get blamed for it, then they overreact in the other direction. A central bank is somewhat insulated from that, I think, because they have other responsibilities, and they're forced to look at it in the context of what the economy needs, not just the immediate banking regulation standpoint. I think they're in a better position to regulate, but that's a long-standing position I've had, and I don't think anything has happened to change that.

2

A View from North America

E. Gerald Corrigan

At the May 2009 plenary meeting of the Trilateral Commission, I presented the following observations to the Commission on the subject of the global economic crisis at that time:

Legacy of the Crisis

The necessary and unprecedented scale of central bank and government intervention—particularly in the United States—triggered by the current economic crisis brings with it material medium-term risks of higher inflation and a persistently larger role of the government in economic and financial affairs that threatens to crowd out private investment and, worse, private initiative.

For this reason, it is not too early to focus considerable and realistic attention on the specifics of exit strategies that will wind-down these official interventions as circumstances permit.

Exit Strategies

On the central bank side, exit strategies will—to an extent—be relatively easy because elements of the rise in central banks' balance sheets will be self-liquidating over time.

In the United States, at least, the wind-down of double-digit deficits and federal spending levels relative to GDP that are well in excess of long-term experience will be extraordinarily difficult to achieve even as growth returns.

For a period of at least the next several years, the welcome rise of the U.S. personal savings rate is likely to be more than offset by the significant rise in government dis-savings, thus leaving the United States with a continuing and potentially large negative savings rate.

Repercussions

The understandable political backlash of the crisis directed at Wall Street brings with it an element of concern that badly needed reforms could result in regulatory overkill that might compromise the financial intermediation process in ways that could undermine long-term economic performance.

As a result of the crisis, the long-standing leadership position of the United States on economic and financial affairs has been badly damaged.

Although this setback is likely to be at least partially reversed over time, the setback will complicate further the already complicated task of strengthening international economic and financial policy coordination.

One Year Later:
Further Insights into Causes and Aftermath of the Crisis

Now, one year later, it is very clear that the scale and duration of official interventions—including de facto governmental ownership and control of a number of financial institutions—are, if anything, greater than had been appreciated during the darkest days of the crisis.

It also appears that winding down such governmental intervention will be more difficult and more time-consuming than many observers expected. That will certainly be the case for the two U.S. housing agencies.

Causes

It is now very clear that in the United States and across other jurisdictions the overwhelming majority of write-downs and losses at financial institutions can be traced to traditional lending activities in such areas as housing, credit cards, commercial real estate, and leveraged finance.

Securitizations of poor-quality assets compounded the nature and incidence of problems growing out of poor lending decisions.

Aftermath

It is now very clear that in virtually all jurisdictions troubled financial institutions were able to raise more private capital and to raise such capital faster than many observers expected at the time of the darkest days of the crisis.

It is estimated that in the past two years such institutions raised more than $700 billion in capital from nongovernmental sources and that the vast majority of such capital was raised in the private capital markets.

In the United States it now appears that taxpayer losses growing out of activities related to the Troubled Asset Relief Program (TARP) may be materially lower than once expected although considerable uncertainties remain regarding repayment prospects in the auto sector, the two housing agencies, and AIG.

On the whole, and recognizing that major uncertainties remain, the recovery in credit markets, including both investment-grade and high-yield bond markets, has been more rapid and more broadly based than many observers expected.

While the recovery in credit markets is welcome, there is a question as to whether the turnaround in credit markets reflects, to some extent, shortened memories as to the lessons associated with the underpricing of credit risk in the period leading up to the crisis.

Finally, and of particular importance, the recovery in global economic activity to date has been somewhat stronger than many observers had expected.

Having said that, it is also true that economic and financial conditions remain somewhat fragile. One source of such fragility is the advent of very serious and immediate debt problems in one or more countries in Europe.

Summary of Major Financial Reforms

Table 1, on the next four pages, provides a summary of important financial reforms that are under discussion in mid-2010.

Table 1. Summary of Major Financial Reforms under Consideration, mid-2010

Subject matter	Jurisdiction	Probability	Status
1. Substantially higher capital requirements via Basel Committee	Most advanced countries	Virtually certain	Lengthy implementation schedule, with full implementation likely sometime in late 2011 or 2012
			Many technical and policy questions yet to be resolved
2. Substantially more rigorous liquidity requirements	Most advanced countries	Virtually certain	Implementation of liquidity standards will be linked to capital requirements
			Many technical and policy questions yet to be resolved
3. Systemic regulator or board	Most advanced countries	Virtually certain	Considerable uncertainty as to role of systemic regulator
			Important differences from country to country

(table continued on next page)

Table 1. Summary of Major Financial Reforms under Consideration, mid-2010 *(continued)*

Subject matter	Jurisdiction	Probability	Status
4. Direct regulation and related reforms of derivatives markets	Most advanced countries	Virtually certain, but with important differences from country to country	Many open questions on details but CCP clearing of standardized contracts and higher margin, capital, and/ or collateral requirements (especially for nonstandard contracts) virtually certain
			May have important implications for some classes of structured products
5. Some form of Volcker Rule	High on reform agenda in United States	Virtually certain to be enacted in United States; outlook in other jurisdictions uncertain	Many details to be worked out in United States by regulators and Systemic Risk Council
			Potentially important cross-border competitive implications

(table continued on next page)

Table 1. Summary of Major Financial Reforms under Consideration, mid-2010 *(continued)*

Subject matter	Jurisdiction	Probability	Status
6. Measures to eliminate too-big-to-fail, including enhanced resolution authority	Under active consideration in United States, United Kingdom, and continental Europe	Highly likely in jurisdictions hardest hit by crisis	Potential for major differences from country to country
			Poorly designed or executed approach could become source of renewed uncertainty and instability
7. Official oversight of extreme downside contingencies and stress tests for systemically important institutions (that is, living wills)	Particular focus in countries hardest hit by the crisis and at systemically important institutions having a cross-border footprint	Highly likely	Large number of open conceptual and execution issues
			Implies major changes in philosophy of prudential supervision
			Cross-border implications raise very difficult policy questions
8. In response to the request of the G-20, the IMF is evaluating the merits of a dual framework of "financial taxes" including a "financial stability contribution" and a "financial activities tax"	Approach contemplates that both "taxes" would be levied in most (if not all) of the G-20 countries	Highly unlikely that such taxes will be widely implemented across G-20 countries; but in some countries including the United States, United Kingdom, and Germany some form of financial tax is highly likely to be implemented	Major outstanding issues as to size and incidence of such taxes
			Some suggestions to the effect that an ex-ante "financial stability contribution" could aggravate moral hazard problems

(table continued on next page)

Table 1. Summary of Major Financial Reforms under Consideration, mid-2010 *(continued)*

Subject matter	Jurisdiction	Probability	Status
9. Enhanced oversight of risk monitoring and risk management.	Most countries	Virtually certain	Starting points across individual institutions difficult to calibrate
			Could entail very costly technology and infrastructure outlays at some institutions
10. Heightened regulation of consumer protection	High-priority item in United States; uncertain outlook in other countries	Virtually certain	Significant differences between House and Senate in the United States
11. Reforms in the credit-rating process	High priority in countries hardest hit by the crisis	Highly likely	Substantially uncertain as to the specifics

Selected Economic and Financial Indicators

Although world GDP growth in 2010 and 2011 is likely to be quite re-spectable (see Table 2), such growth is driven largely by Asia generally and by China and India particularly.

- Higher growth in Asia raises the question of whether relative pat-terns of growth will bring with them greater economic power in fast-growth countries, especially China, with spillover implications for foreign policy and geopolitical considerations more generally.

- Notwithstanding the promising vision of the G-20, it remains to be seen whether enhanced international cooperation in economic and financial policy will be achieved.

In the mature industrial countries, including the United States, growth prospects in 2010 and 2011 are not likely to be sufficient to materially reduce very high unemployment rates, with all that implies in economic and political terms.

It is not a surprise that the virtual explosion in government deficits in most countries, especially the major industrial countries, has alarming medium-term implications even if medium-term growth is sustained at or near potential GDP growth rates. Figure 1 provides some perspective on this situation in the United States.

- Both gross and net financing requirements will, at some point in the medium term, have to be reduced substantially in order to limit the risk of crowding out private investment and private incentive in a setting in which sooner or later governmental financing burdens could result in substantial upward pressures on interest rates.

- It will require an extraordinary amount of political will—and perhaps some good luck—in order to bring such deficits into line with historical experience even over the long run.

Similar pressures are evident in the sharp increases in government debt-to-GDP ratios in many countries.

Although the profiles of current account positions are not today as bad as they were in the period leading up to the crisis, the size of the surplus in China is noteworthy, as is the size of the deficit in the United States.

- Note also that (1) symptoms of real estate price pressures and (2) the risk of a rise in asset quality problems in the Chinese banking system cannot be ignored.

Table 2. Selected Economic and Financial Indicators for Selected Countries and Areas, 2010

Country or area	Real GDP growth % year on year		Unemployment %	Gov't balance % GDP		Current acc't % GDP	Gov't debt % GDP		10-yr. gov't bond yld %
	2010	2011(est.)	Most recent	2005	2010	2010	2005	2010	as of April 29, 2010
United States	2.7	2.5	9.7	-3.2	-9.7	-3.3	61.3	92.8[a]	3.77
Japan	2.4	1.8	4.9	-4.3	-10.6	2.4	191.1	227.8	1.29
United Kingdom	1.7	3.3	8.0	-3.0	-11.7	-0.3	41.5	64.7	3.95
Canada	3.2	2.8	8.2	1.6	-1.8	-2.0	58.5	NA	3.67
France	2.5	2.6	10.1	-3.0	-8.9	-2.0	66.4	84.8	3.33
Germany	2.3	2.4	7.5	-3.3	-5.6	3.5	68.1	79.3	3.06
Italy	1.5	1.9	8.5	-4.3	-5.3	-2.2	105.8	117.1	4.08
Euro area	1.7	2.2	10.0	-2.6	-7.0	0.1	70.1	84.7	3.06
Greece	-0.1	0.7	10.2	-5.2	-8.7	-9.0	111.0	120.4	9.06
Spain	-0.3	1.4	19.0	1.0	-10.2	-2.7	43.0	66.6	4.07
Ireland	-2.5	1.0	13.2	1.7	-11.6	0.6	27.1	77.9	5.12
Portugal	0.7	0.9	10.3	-6.1	-8.3	-9.7	63.6	86	5.49
Brazil	6.4	5.0	7.2	-3.4	-3.5	-3.0	46.5	41	4.89
Russia	5.8	6.1	7.9	7.6	-2.0	5.6	15.7	7.9	6.05
India	8.2	8.7	9.5	-7.0	-8.0	-2.5	79.1	78.0	8.09
China	11.4	10.0	4.2	-1.2	-1.9	5.3	17.9	22.2	3.43
World	4.8	4.8	—	-1.2	-5.9	—	—	—	—

Source: Goldman Sachs Research.

Note: Data completed at the end of April 2010. All forward-looking data assume that the European debt crisis will be contained.

a In the interest of comparability, includes certain classes of debt of state and local governments.

Figure 1. U.S. Government Receipts and Outlays, 1946–2009

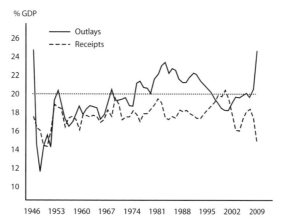

Source: Goldman Sachs Research.

- Also noteworthy is the combination of large budget deficits and large current account deficits in Greece and Portugal.

Risk Factors Going Forward

Is the changing pattern of economic growth and power likely to result in a more or less permanent reduction in the geopolitical influence of the United States and Europe?

Is there a material risk that the medium- to longer-term outlook for budget deficits in many countries will impede economic growth and job creation, thus planting the seeds for renewed economic and financial instability?

Will the financial reform agenda materially reduce the probabilities of major financial shocks while preserving the essential efficiency of the global financial intermediation process?

Has the philosophy of economic and financial "capitalism" been permanently compromised; if so, what are the implications of that outcome?

3

A View from Europe

Sir Callum McCarthy

The questions for discussion in this session are wide ranging. I intend to concentrate on whether what has happened to date makes it significantly less likely that we will face a repetition of the financial and economic crisis that the world faced—and make only obiter dicta on other questions. And I shall approach these questions from the experience—the painful experience—of someone who was involved in the regulatory issues and practices that have contributed to our present difficulties. Thus, I have a particular view on the central banking and regulatory proposals that have been advanced in order to avoid a repetition of our present travails.

Avoiding a Repetition of the Current Crisis

No one is in any doubt about how close to the edge of the precipice the world came economically in October 2008, when what had initially been a problem of liquidity, then solvency in financial institutions became a general question of confidence, and then spilled over from finance into the real economy with frightening speed and impact. As Mervyn King aptly summarized the position: global equity markets fell more sharply in one month than in any month in history; Chinese electricity consumption, which had been growing at 15 percent per annum, fell in November by 8 percent on a year earlier; car sales in Brazil fell by a quarter on a year before; in Japan, November industrial production fell 8.5 percent on a year before; in Germany, exports fell by 10 percent; in the United States a million jobs were lost in the last two months of 2008. The impact was worldwide: in the United States; in the European Union; in Japan; in Brazil, Russia, India, and China—the BRIC countries.

The cost has been immense—in terms of lost output (the reduction from the trend growth worldwide has been twice that of the recession of the 1980s); in terms of the cost of government intervention (now estimated to be in excess of $11 trillion for the financial sector); in terms of the resulting indebtedness of governments (the UK's position, where national debt has risen during the past two years from 30 to 80 percent of GDP and annual borrowing from 3 to 12 percent, is only one example of the deterioration in the fiscal position of many countries). The price of recovering from what has occurred will have to be paid, via lower economic growth, higher taxes, and lower public services, for many years to come. This, rather than the direct cost of government intervention to support the banks, large though the latter has been, is the real cost of the near disaster.

I start with this bleak reminder for two reasons. First, I believe the relief we all share in not having fallen into the abyss we faced in the fourth quarter of 2008 has made us underestimate the continuing fragility of the present position, which remains acutely dangerous. And, second, it is against this scale of near disaster and continuing acute danger that we have to judge the response to date. Does what has been proposed match the scale of the danger?

I am afraid that my reply is that what has been proposed to date by way of reform to the regulation of financial firms largely fails to match the task.

Let me explain why.

Much of what has been proposed in the financial regulation space by way of remedies is likely to be ineffective. For example:

- It is fashionable to claim that the problems arose from inadequate corporate governance, and much attention—in, for example, David Walker's admirable report in the UK on corporate governance[1]—has been devoted to how to get better boards. In one—tautological— sense, boards that make bad decisions are bad boards. The problem, however, is that there is little evidence either anecdotal or systematic to link board composition with good (or bad) decisions. In the UK, for example, one bank had an exemplary board: the chairman of its asset and liability committee was a distinguished ex-banker, its senior director an experienced businessman who had served on the Court of the Bank of England, and its other non-executive directors included a very successful fund manager, the finance director of a publicly quoted private equity firm, and a partner in a Big Four

---

1 David Walker, *A Review of Corporate Governance in UK Banks and Other Financial Industry Entities: Final Recommendations* (London: The Walker Review Secretariat, November 26, 2009).

accounting firm. That bank was Northern Rock. I could give other examples to illustrate why improving corporate governance and revamping board selection are unlikely to provide the solution.

- Nor do I believe that the answer is to be found in further regulation of hedge funds and private equity, as many in Europe seem to believe. The unpalatable reality is that this crisis originated in the most central and most regulated part of the financial system, namely banks; and for the most part it was associated with poor credit decisions and poor liquidity management, the two most central (and historic) skill sets required of banks. Action on hedge funds is largely an irrelevance.

- Nor is the answer to be found in the reordering of regulatory organizations. There have been mistakes aplenty in regulatory policy and supervisory practices, some very publicly acknowledged, others swept under the carpet. But they are not confined to one model of regulation. They have occurred in countries that have a mixture of principles and rules (as in the UK), and in countries and institutions that were much more rules based (as in the United States). There have been failings in those countries where central banks had responsibility for supervision and in countries where central banking and supervision were separated. So, again, I think that to seek the answer in reorganizing regulatory institutions will prove of marginal value. Some of those changes, which will represent a move toward the separate regulation of overlapping financial sectors, will actually be harmful as they will increase the opportunity for regulatory arbitrage and the danger that there will be a stimulus for growth in the nonregulated sectors.

- And I would add that, while I agree of course with all those who say we need better supervisors—more thoughtful, more dynamic, harder working—I have yet to hear any proposal as to how to achieve this in practice. La Fontaine's fable is apposite: we can all agree on belling the cat; it's just that no one knows how to do it. And aspirations without practical proposals on how to achieve them remain just that—wishful thinking.

There are proposals that address more relevantly the real causes of the crisis. In this category I include:

- The working of the Basel Committee to recalculate the capital that banks must hold, particularly against trading activities. This is something that is clearly necessary, as the assumptions about the effectiveness of risk management made by both the banks and their supervisors and the methodology, with its overreliance on mathematical techniques and on ratings from the rating agencies that both shared, have been found wanting.

- The emphasis on liquidity management rather than on capital, which is now coming to the fore.

- The new recognition in the Group of Twenty and the Financial Stability Board (FSB) of the need to go beyond the Group of Seven and include other countries, notably India and China.

- The effort being devoted, particularly in Europe, to limit the externalities associated with a bank failure by establishing systems that make it easier to transfer the business of a failing bank to other banks, colloquially known as "living wills." This is clearly desirable but will require great administrative and systems efforts to make it work, and it has major implications for requiring a step change in simplifying the corporate structure of banking groups. It, like other proposals, will take some years to implement.

- The encouragement being given to the use of clearinghouses and exchanges for the trading of derivatives, notably in the United States where Tim Geithner as Treasury secretary is continuing the efforts that he made when at the New York Fed with the Financial Services Authority to tackle the problems of settlement of derivatives.

All these will help. But they fall very significantly short of dealing with some major flaws in the consensus that has driven best practice in central banking and regulation over the last decade. Unless we face the scale of the task of righting these mistakes—in a way in which we have not yet done—we will not succeed in making the changes needed to avoid a repetition, no doubt in some new and unexpected form, of what has occurred. The issues that need addressing include:

- We need to reexamine whether inflation targeting—measured against an increasingly narrow definition of inflation—can continue to be given the preeminent position it has enjoyed. It is far from clear that central banks that took the credit for the low retail price index inflation that was such a feature of the years of the great moderation recognized the relative importance of their own decisions on interest rates and of the beneficial supply-side shock from the advent of India, China, and other countries as suppliers. It is clear that the concentration on an inflation target, and the explicit rejection of responsibility for movements in asset prices—a policy eloquently advanced in the United States by the Federal Reserve, but widely shared—is no longer tenable. The results of this policy have been too damaging.

- But if central banks are to assume responsibility for limiting asset bubbles, they will have to have weapons at their disposal other than interest rate movements. There is no agreement as to what these should be: quantitative controls on particular forms of credit growth is an option; dynamic provisioning, by which the capital required to be held by banks would be adjusted up or down depending on where it was judged the economic cycle had reached, is another. But common to all the options is a blurring of the distinction between monetary policy on the one hand and regulatory policy on the other—the first aimed at macroeconomic objectives, the latter aimed at controlling individual institutions, each one considered separately. It is a change in approach that will require quite fundamental rethinking of central bank responsibilities, corporate governance, and even independence.

- There are questions of size in relation to the size of both individual institutions and the financial sector as a whole; questions that have begun to be addressed in part, but are far from resolution. Should there be a limit to the size of any bank—in terms of its size either relative to competitors, or relative to the economy in which it operates, or relative to the economy in which it is headquartered? And, if there is a policy objective here, how is it to be implemented? (The IMF and Basel Committee are beginning to address this.) More fundamentally, should we seek to limit the size of the financial sector in any country relative to that country's GDP? We know from the Icelandic experience the problems (still unresolved) that a very large banking sector relative to a country's size can cause. But Iceland's banks had assets that were nearly 10 times the country's GDP; the ratio for Switzerland is more than 6, and for the UK 4 1/2 (these are OECD figures; I have seen estimates that are much higher). Are we prepared to accept these ratios? And what mechanism is available to restrain them if we decide that restraint is sensible?

- Last, I should flag up a general class of issues that are normally described as accounting issues and, by implication, relegated to a subordinate and technical level. This grossly underestimates their importance. The acute dangers of October 2008 arose from a breakdown in mutual confidence and trust, as no institution believed it could understand the position of any other. Confidence and trust require information on assets that is believable and believed, which in turn requires confidence in the methodology used to identify and measure those assets. This is not a question of data. The latest report and accounts of Citi runs to 272 pages, that of Deutsche Bank to 352, and that of HSBC to 500—all of them, incidentally, at least 5 percent longer than the year before.

But more and more data do not equate to—indeed may militate against—better understanding. We suffer at present from a position that the basic measurement systems are inadequate and lack credibility. There is a fierce argument waging between those who believe that it is essential to use mark-to-market conventions and those who believe that their use has contributed to the creation of misleading impressions and unnecessary pressures. The present compromise—different treatment for assets held on the banking book and for those held on the trading book—has, like many of the accounting conventions adopted, the advantage of some logic and the disadvantage of considerable scope for manipulation. There are many other examples: the Lehman Brothers "Repo 105" is but the most recent. We should recognize that the complexity of modern financial instruments has outstripped our ability to describe them adequately or to understand their effects properly. The solution embedded in much central bank, regulatory, and counterparty risk assessment of relying on someone else—namely the rating agencies—to do this has proved unworkable. But we need to face up to the erosion of confidence that has occurred.

So my answer to the first question we are asked to address is that we have hardly started on the task of rethinking the concepts and beliefs that guided central banks and regulators through the period of the great moderation; that many of the immediate answers that have been given are of marginal relevance; and that the most difficult and important questions remain to be tackled.

More Effective International Order Unlikely in Near Future

Let me turn quickly to the other questions we were asked to address. I confess to quite severe scepticism about the effectiveness of efforts to establish a more effective international order, for a number of reasons.

Some are technical. The new and welcome emphasis on liquidity, for example, as a key risk measure and control for banks will for good technical reasons (the differing policy toward eligible collateral by central banks being one) be determined by currency group, so that there will be a Eurozone policy, a U.S. policy, and a UK policy rather than an international policy.

More broadly, there is the reality, emphasized by the events of the last two years, that it is national governments and taxpayers who have the resources to intervene in the first instance in a crisis. Two things flow from this, both of which hinder international cooperation. First, there is a continuing reticence on the part of national authorities to be candid about the position of major financial institutions for which they are responsible, even with well-regarded counterparties—central banks and supervisors—in other countries in which those institutions operate on a major scale and where the institutions' activities can significantly affect financial stability. As the problems of banks mutated and intensified in 2008, very few national authorities—the Swiss being a shining exception—showed the willingness to discuss their banks' problems with the degree of candor required if international rather than national solutions are to work. I would be surprised if this has significantly changed.

Second, there is a transmission problem: how to translate a view, if one is reached within an international body (IMF or FSB at the global level or the ESRC within the EU), into action by those within individual countries who are responsible for supervision and whose taxpayers eventually have to meet the cost of failure of fiscal, monetary, and regulatory policies. The precedents of the IMF Financial Sector Assessment Program and the EU stability and growth pact are not encouraging. But without an effective transmission mechanism, the new macroprudential organizations run the risk of being at best high-quality think tanks, without effective means of translating their recommendations into practice.

I think it important that attempts to develop international solutions recognize these problems, rather than proceeding by ignoring them. They are too important for that.

My overall conclusions are that we have only started—and not necessarily on the right lines in all instances—on the immense task of identifying the failings in the thinking that guided policy in central banks and regulators during the period of the great moderation. I have attempted to identify some of the residual issues of major importance that the needed intellectual rebuilding will have to address. But if we do not recognize the scale of the task, we are unlikely to bring forward changes that either match the scale of the risks that still so clearly continue to exist or are equal to the task of preventing a recurrence of the present near disaster.

4

A View from Pacific Asia

Naoki Tanaka

Business cycles changed with dizzying speed right after the Lehman Brothers shock hit the world. Business firms, feeling as if demand had evaporated in an instant, at first began squeezing inventory, resulting in the disappearance of unintentional stocks from Japan in a matter of some six months. Production rebounded subsequently and kept rising for twelve months in a row.

Still output of quite a few industrial sectors stayed at no more than 80 percent of the pre-Lehman level. It is interesting that expectations have not grown sufficiently on financial functions for averting future risks. Demand for securitized products, once touted for their risk-dispersing effects, has run dry, and demand has stayed sluggish ever since despite the real economy's recovery to some 80 percent of the precrisis level.

Two reasons explain why the securitization business has remained stagnant. One is that preconditions have yet to be met for the stable price formation of securitized products. The other reason is that tighter regulatory rules are in the works. The emphasis of proposed regulations varies between the United States and the European Union (EU), and no easy agreement appears in sight even at such forums as the Group of Seven, Bank for International Settlements (BIS), and the Group of Twenty. For potential buyers of securitized products, this can mean unexpected fluctuations in prices and raise concerns if the market has liquidity enough to smoothly digest buy and sell orders.

Behind impaired price formation is the lingering uncertainty that collateralized debt obligations (CDOs) and mortgage-backed securities (MBSs) could flood the market at any time. Such securities have been bought in large volumes by the U.S. Federal Reserve Board and the European Central Bank (ECB) to the extent of bloating their balance sheets, and a release of those securities onto the market could occur if the central banks decide to implement an exit strategy. If transparency in the price-formation process is to be improved, a central bank needs to announce beforehand a schedule for selling such securities from its portfolio.

Central banks are, however, running into difficulty in unloading their securitized products. They anticipate the near inevitability of one sovereign state after another being compelled to refinance their government bonds. The countries' financial situations have been severely impacted by massive issues of government bonds aimed at easing the Lehman shock. In the United States, the spread between the yield on ten-year Treasury bonds and the short-term interest rate was nearing the historic level of around 4 percent in the early days of last April. If the ongoing economic recovery gains momentum, the spread will likely widen further. In addition, when a widening spread in the United States is coupled with the Fed's unloading of securitized products, concern should rise in one stroke over a possible crunch of money markets. This is why the Fed carefully avoids making reference to an exit strategy.

New Tools Being Tapped to
Overcome Stagnant Financial Functions

Since January 2010 when President Barack Obama in announced a proposed package of financial regulatory measures, dubbed the Volcker Rule, the White House has clarified its policy for imposing strict regulations on the operations of financial institutions to avoid repeating the nightmare of the capital markets shut off from liquidity.

Let me discuss here only the aspect of international consistency of the proposed regulations. For more than a quarter of a century, the United States has made up its current-account deficits with capital account surpluses. This meant that the ranks of buyers of securitized products that originated in the United States ultimately had spread around the world. Sale of such securitized products had been brokered not only by leading U.S. investment banks and commercial banks but also by major European financial institutions. Those financial companies had purchased subprime loans, and other loan claims originated in the United States as part of the financial products they marketed and repackaged into CDOs.

With excess investment built in, the U.S. economy has needed external finance as an indispensable ingredient, and private sector financial institutions of the world have offered deficit financing of massive proportions to the United States. This led to the birth of the business of originating and distributing MBSs. MBSs then were repackaged into CDOs for easier purchase by investors. The Lehman shock meant that the value chain management of the securitized business collapsed entirely. Since September 2008, the entities that came to absorb shocks in fact have been limited to sovereign states. They were engrossed in underpinning their domestic economic activities by ignoring the widening deficits in their public finances. In this process, it became clear that a major difference existed in the workings of the United States and the EU.

More than half of all U.S. dollars issued are held overseas, but the responsibility to manage the dollar still rests with the United States, the sovereign state. In contrast, the duty to manage the euro is in the hands of the ECB, which keeps an arm's length from the decision-making process of EU-member sovereign states. Even in the midst of the ongoing Greek crisis, which has brought the issue of sovereign risk to the fore, the ECB has failed to play even the role of second fiddle.

The Volcker Plan calls for reviewing regulations of financial institutions with the determination not to repeat the "too big to fail" bailout experience. It will likely lead to an examination of financial institutions from the following two viewpoints: (1) Will financial institutions be able to continue to finance the U.S. federal deficits? (2) Will they be able to build up the value chain themselves? The EU for its part is expected to present a third viewpoint: (3) Can the Volcker plan have an international consistency?

Fundamental reviews begun in various quarters, as seen above, explain why a recovery of the securitization business will take some time. Business firms will again face the important question of hedging risks by using the futures markets. A new proposition has also emerged for business firms in terms of overcoming the instability of prices. While they are supposed to serve as a yardstick for resource distribution, prices have been rendered instable in the wake of the stagnation hitting securitized products. The lesson for business firms to learn here is that it will not suffice for them to simply demand financial functions.

The emissions trading markets, born in the EU, also have been in rough waters. The idea was that carbon prices set by the futures markets for emissions rights should provide a yardstick for moves to stimulate carbon-reduction research and development efforts. However, the belief that resource distribution can be improved by prices born out of securitization inevitably has lost its magnetism, albeit temporarily.

In the realization that they cannot completely steer clear of future risks, business firms and others have begun tackling specific methods for stemming risks one by one. For example, in April 2010, the Tokyo metropolitan government began imposing total volume controls on greenhouse-gas emissions from commercial buildings in Japan's capital. It also started brokering emissions transactions. Tokyo also signed cross-regional tie-up agreements with Hokkaido, Aomori, Iwate, Akita, and Yamagata prefectures to receive supplies of renewable energy from those northern regions. The arrangements, for example, will open the way for commercial buildings in Tokyo to, for a fee, use wind power generated by these mountainous, idyllic prefectures. These moves can be a harbinger of measures to cope with future risks by the use of new tools, without awaiting the birth of futures markets. They are also indications of the real economy stepping out of the stagnancy that has plagued financial functions.

Dispersing Risk in Bipolarized World Takes Cooperation

In the eighteen months since the Lehman shock, three propositions in regard to financial affairs have completely disappeared or are on the verge of doing so. Proposition one: Monetary policy, above all central banks' supply of funds, should be determined according to the size of the deflationary gap. Proposition two: To prevent systemic risk from spreading to the international community, uniform control by the Bank for International Settlements should apply to banks that conduct international operations. Proposition three: In confronting risks pertaining to their financial markets, industrialized countries should tap into the pool of know-how their financial institutions have built up.

Conventional wisdom had it that dispersing risk is the foremost prerequisite for fund management, making it extremely important to pinpoint where risks lie. Countries that achieved a high degree of industrial development thus were considered best suited to exercise their forte of spotting risks. The criterion of the day was that developing countries would do well by turning to the wealth of intelligence accumulated by advanced countries in dealing with the practical job of capital accumulation. In this view, the dissemination of financial knowledge and methods flowed from developed to developing countries. It was not thought that challenges tackled by developing countries would lead to new propositions. Conventional wisdom, however, has been upended.

The crumbling of the first proposition had very much to do with microprudential policy, under which monetary authorities issue inspection guidelines to banks to maintain the stability of the credit mechanism. It became apparent that this kind of tightening alone was unable to control the great waves of the economy that at times led to the creation of bubbles.

When major advanced countries began implementing the kind of macroeconomic policies that spawned the great moderation period, the initial upshot was the appearance of the so-called easy money–induced stock market upswing that occurred amid an economic slump. When risk aversion wore away in the face of high-flying stock markets, a bubble began building—an experience the global economy was exposed to from 2001 to 2006.

The great moderation occurred first in Japan and then in the United States. This was the result of the lopsided pressures that were put on the respective economies so that they would be managed to achieve the great moderation. The Bank of Japan (BOJ) had to promise that it would continue its accommodative policy until it became sure of achieving positive price increases year on year. When it made this commitment, the "policy duration effect" materialized. Simply put, all market participants and economic entities—everyone—came to believe that there was no possibility of credit tightening for the foreseeable future.

This created a risk-profile distortion field. How soon would risk appear? To what degree would it surface? No one knew. So they placed big bets, and the bubble expanded.

At the same time, something called the yen-carry trade emerged. Investors took out low-interest-rate yen loans, took the money to the foreign exchange market, then used the foreign currency to make overseas investments.

All this was made possible by a BOJ intent on conquering deflation. Maintaining the policy meant injecting unlimited amounts of funds into the economy. Deflation, after all, was a result of a worsening in Japan's supply-demand balance.

As for the second proposition, financial regulators around the world kept a vigilant eye on individual banks, focusing on the size and quality of their assets. In a strong economy, banks' loan-loss reserves are reduced almost to nil, making their equity capital adequate to the extent of inducing the banks to build up their lending assets.

With the collapse of the bubble, however, a process of reciprocity began in which banks' balance sheets were synchronized to business fluctuations, and increased loan losses led to the erosion of equity capital, forcing the banks to decrease lending assets.

BIS regulations set standards for microprudence, aimed at ensuring the health of individual banks. But when systemic risk reared up, the regulations paradoxically turned out to be a destabilizing factor in the macroprudence domain. In the same way as the International Monetary Fund (IMF) fell from grace for its failure to come up with any macroprudence standards, the BIS had its prestige bruised by trying to introduce equity ratio regulations without sufficient consideration of reciprocity.

The IMF and World Bank tackled institutionalizing an economic management model based on the market economy system for the world as a whole, supposedly building up a practical framework called the Washington consensus—only to see it crumble. For its part, the BIS was supposed to have completed a traditional system of banks conducting mutual surveillance of one another based on practical banking operations, but at the end of the day it also failed to make the grade for offering a useful framework.

The third proposition means an abrupt tidal shift in how financial techniques are applied.

Conventional wisdom had it that the financial industry was something that was handled only in advanced countries and only by their major financial institutions. These institutions were supposed to have their armies of experienced professionals develop new financial products and explore new ways to market those products.

Then a major wave of securitization, which was supposed to make financial markets more efficient, washed over the industry. Things did not quite go in that direction. As fiscal deficits rapidly grew following the Lehman shock, moves to measure sovereign risks and streamline a framework to avoid the worsening of these risks gained traction. There were even calls to regulate credit default swaps.

A bipolarization set in: on one end, sovereign states in the industrialized world intensified their mutual cooperation; on the other end, investors and financial companies turned to setting up explicit futures positions.

So what is the outlook? It will be important for the sovereign state to rein in the risk takers who set up short positions on futures markets. If states can effectively control these risk takers, if they can cooperate, they should be able to open an avenue for cutting expenses.

Nations Look to New International Order

Remarkable changes in presumptions for observing what is happening to the world economy have occurred in the eighteen months since the collapse of Lehman Brothers Holdings Inc. in the United States.

These changes signify the emergence of new phenomena: (1) Emerging nations have started immense efforts to pursue independence and self-reliance; (2) a drastic review has been undertaken of the commitments made to economic growth by industrial countries; and (3) the world is seeking an architect of a new global governance system and is pursuing a theoretical paradigm for a new international order.

There is no question that the once-dominant economic orthodoxy based on free market principles and the pursuit of democracy is dead. This concept, referred to as the Washington consensus, was recommended by the U.S. government and Washington, D.C.–based financial organizations as a yardstick by which the success of development in underdeveloped nations is measured.

When it comes to the influence exerted on a new international economic order by major industrial nations, the world's geopolitical landscape has been dramatically redrawn.

As for Japan, it has a serious problem on its hands as it remains indecisive about creating a national consensus-building mechanism to determine the basics of diplomacy to adapt to the changing world order.

When the subprime mortgage crisis exposed systemic risks in global financial systems, such phenomena affected the United States and the EU in distinctly different ways.

In the United States, buyers virtually disappeared from the market for securitized products, which quickly stymied the flow of credit and paralyzed a broad range of financial services from consumer loans, to lease contracts, to provision of scholarships — and, needless to add, mortgage loans.

A dramatic rise in mortgage delinquencies triggered concern over the probability of default on synthetic CDOs that are backed by subprime mortgages, causing the entire financial system to stop working.

Because the general patterns of investment and consumption by Americans are closely intertwined with financial market trends, the impact of the financial crisis was evidently strong in the household sector. U.S. demand for durable goods surprisingly seems to have halved instantaneously amid the crisis.

Economists often pointed out that U.S. household consumption was too high, making up a disproportionately large percentage of the nation's gross domestic product (GDP). In fact, the trend gave the impression that their demand shrank extremely in the wake of the financial crisis.

Meanwhile, European countries have become less risk averse in their investments owing to the spillover effect of low U.S. interest rates on the region's economy.

Excessive investment in housing, including resort facilities, grew at a phenomenal pace, so monetary authorities could not find any means to rein in the investment boom.

But the asset bubble was not caused by nature; it was caused by excessive economic behaviors.

Ireland was once known as the Celtic Tiger because of its stellar economic growth. The high growth period was supported partly by the blistering speed of expansion in that nation's information technology (IT) sector. Before that, Ireland was one of the poorest countries in Europe and had a long history of emigration, supplying cheap labor to the world.

As the globalization of financial services has proceeded apace around the world, the Irish capital of Dublin was sometimes touted as one of the major international financial centers because of its proximity to the City of London, the world's largest financial hub.

The situation in Iceland is a bit different from Ireland. The IT industry is the ideal business activity for a tiny nation like Iceland because growth in this sector is driven chiefly by advanced network technologies. IT firms are able to flexibly consolidate their service areas or separate some of them.

In contrast, durable-goods manufacturing initially requires a certain level of market depth and breadth for growth.

How did the small island nation create such a vast asset bubble? The simple answer is that the bubble originally arose as a result of the Internet boom of the late 1990s, fueled in part by global efforts to address the Y2K (Year 2000) switchover.

In the EU, the systemic risk problem manifested itself in refinancing difficulties that banks faced.

In the region, where financial institutions are allowed to handle both commercial banking and investment banking operations under the universal banking system, a slowdown in refinancing operations by the ECB heightened concern over the quality of banks' asset holdings. In

August 2007, Jean-Claude Trichet, president of the ECB, was forced to pump seemingly unlimited liquidity into banks of eurozone nations.

While the United States and the EU were proceeding with economic consolidations, Japan faced the challenge of addressing steep falls in production as a result of rapid progress in inventory cuts by manufacturers in all sectors, which put in place supply chain management systems worldwide.

As such, every industrial nation is struggling to tackle medium-term consolidation.

Insulating Economies

In the meantime, such emerging nations as China, India, and Brazil have taken measures to insulate their own economies from the impact of a global downturn, while carefully reexamining their growth targets.

As a result, China and India maintained their trend rates of growth in 2009, while Brazil managed to avoid negative growth last year.

If the decoupling theory proves to be right—an indication that emerging-market economies have decoupled from developed nations' economic cycles—industrial nations will pale in comparison to emerging nations.

For instance, the economic increment in emerging nations, relative to the world's economic growth between 2008 and 2011, is likely to be nearly double that for industrial countries. The trend suggests that if firms in developed nations really want to boost sales, they will have to sharpen their focus on emerging markets.

The gap in the growth outlook for the two clubs is a primary factor behind the changing geopolitical landscape.

To counter the global crisis, developed countries injected a great amount of liquidity into their banking systems and, on top of that, scurried to implement massive stimulus packages while turning a blind eye to burgeoning government deficits.

Concern over each government's ability to fund its deficit as well as high levels of public debt have brought the risk of sovereign defaults to the fore. The situation now is such that the government of a sovereign state is about to come in conflict with the market.

In January 2010, discussion about Greece, which is teetering on the brink of financial collapse, heated up among EU leaders. Because Greece needs to refinance large chunks of sovereign debt in the coming months, the primary concern for the nation is investors' response to new bond issues.

For now, Greece's debt problem poses enormous challenges for the EU member states most exposed to sovereign risks as well as rich European nations. However, the EU's rescue package for Greece, if finalized, could mean that the EU will have no choice but to use most of the financial and other resources that were initially set aside for the region's engagement with the international community to help Greece and other member states.

That assumption should impose a sort of restraint on consideration about who or which entity should play a role as orchestrator of global governance for tomorrow.

Policy Persuasion

As for Japan, there is a high possibility that the government will be persuaded to change its policy basics through its dialogue with the market. In the worst case, Japan may be spurned by the market's cold response. These situations illustrate that the government has been forced into a tight corner by potential sovereign risk.

To face up to the harsh reality of the market, there is indeed no choice but to carry out reforms in a way that seems most appropriate to harnessing the real value of the nation's assets inherent in people's skills, expertise, and technology.

This means that in these tough times, it may be businesspeople, university students, and concerned citizens—not politicians—who think seriously about what one can do to pursue a new global governance framework.

In Japan, financial institutions are the main purchasers of and investors in government bonds because Japanese households have a tendency to build up savings rather than invest in government bonds.

Consequently, when management of the accumulated government bonds becomes a serious problem, the nation's financial system is unable to remain intact. If sovereign risks come to the fore, this will immediately threaten financial stability.

Here is the bottom line: Japan should narrowly focus on efforts to help firms improve productivity.

The United States believes that the basic tenet of financial system reform is to avoid going back to the too-big-to-fail doctrine.

Meanwhile, the EU adopts a too-big-to-save approach to banking regulations as there are many European banks whose sizes are out of proportion in terms of each member state's economic scale.

This is why European authorities opted not to conduct stress tests on banks to assess vulnerability in the financial sector, as was the case in the United States. Instead, the EU bases its regulatory principles on the forbearance policy of granting banks time to return to solvency.

Given the fact that financial operations almost entirely came to a halt around the globe, banks will have to spend a lot of time trying to jump-start their businesses.

Japan faces a major challenge of continuing fiscal deficit funding. The tough task ahead for the United States is to press ahead with financial system reforms aimed at maintaining stability and eliminating risks. The EU will be put to the test of its ability to taking advantage of the market to promote overhaul of each member's financial system.

Fiscal Revamp Needed to Avoid Global Crowding-Out

Tax revenues cover less than half of the expenditures in Japan's budget for fiscal 2010, which started in April, and this "half revenue" situation is expected to continue for about two years. The Japanese people cannot rule out the possibility that their country is heading for a fiscal collapse. It is necessary to consider a possible breakdown scenario as a way to avoid such a situation.

The debt crisis in Greece has created a new version of the scenario, which I call "global crowding-out." Private businesses will not be able to borrow money because of the unfavorable international flow of funds.

Let's consider a country that has a huge fiscal deficit. When the economy is recovering, demand for funds from both the private sector and the state grows, causing an unexpected rise in interest rates. Coupon rates of newly issued bonds will rise, and the government has to pay more interest for its refunding bonds, leading to further deterioration of the state's finances. But the government has to procure funds from the market, however high the borrowing cost.

Private companies, in contrast, do not necessarily borrow money at high interest rates. Loans with unfavorable conditions negatively affect the profitability of their investment projects. In addition, soaring interest rates in the initial stage of an economic recovery indicate that the recovery may not be sustainable. Some companies may give up funding, which means they are crowded out. A growing fiscal deficit could be a drag on the economy in this sense, even if the government boosts spending to stimulate the economy.

This theory is based on a closed economy, but, because most countries adopt open economies, it is unlikely that the government and private businesses will compete with each other over funds. A more likely scenario is that the possibility of a government default caused by falling tax revenues will be discussed first, then the creditworthiness of companies—whose loan repayment depends solely on their cash flow—will be examined. That means that even top companies cannot always get better credit ratings than governments. Credit-rating agencies customarily give higher ratings to sovereign states.

Ever since Greece's series of debt management scandals broke in January, players in the financial markets have been taking advantage of the country's slack economic governance. First, they sold Greek bond futures. The yield spread between Greek and German bonds widened rapidly. Greece is not the only European country with poor governance. Many investors think they can also capitalize on Portugal, Spain, and Ireland; and they are looking at governance of a supranational entity: the EU. Investors are establishing short positions against euro futures.

The ECB is not the central bank of a sovereign state. The U.S. Federal Reserve Board and the Bank of Japan have the responsibility and authority to make independent decisions to serve as lenders of last resort. But the ECB cannot do anything before considering how the states will act, just as game theory entails. Each country, also following the rules of game theory, chooses viable options while it monitors reactions from various groups of its citizens. This means the ECB lacks decisiveness, one of the main factors of economic governance. Investors smell honey in the European single currency.

While the euro is widely expected to continue to fall for some time, investors outside the eurozone are likely to make cautious decisions on their investments in countries that adopt the single currency. Even nations with few concerns about fiscal collapse could see foreign investment flee. The year 2010 may be remembered as the year that global crowding-out hit the eurozone.

If global crowding-out takes place in Japan, its impact will be more severe than in Europe because Japanese companies are doing business in a country where the possibility of fiscal breakdown does exist.

A number of Japanese companies and financial institutions have been raising capital through new share issues since 2009, leading to a concern over a supply-demand imbalance in the stock market. If companies get lower credit ratings than the government, the flow of new funds into the corporate sector will fall and investors will sell Japanese shares and leave the country. Global crowding-out may create a vicious cycle in which the private sector has fewer opportunities to do business and tax revenues fall as a result. Crowding-out in an open economy is likely to produce a more radical response than in a closed economy.

The yen is being bought against the backdrop of the euro's decline. That makes some people think that Japan is a popular investment target. But we have to think carefully. It is true that short-term funds are pouring into Japan as a direct response to euro selling, but purchase of short-term government bonds by overseas investors does not help Japanese companies acquire the long-term funds they need. What the government has to do now is draft a road map for fiscal reconstruction in order to prevent global crowding-out from hitting Japan.

Japan's Wrongheaded Policies Sent Economy into Trap

Japan's downfall is no longer an infrequent subject of discussion within the country, with its fading presence in the international community already appearing as a major topic in the domestic media. Why did this happen, and is there a strategy that can lift Japan out of its doldrums?

The Japanese economy has been caught in a trap of wrongheaded economic policies, behind which lies overconfidence in the theory that the level of effective demand can be controlled through the intervention of a sovereign nation into the economic system. To get out of the trap, Japan needs to rethink government intervention and create a mechanism designed to transfer to the current generation some of the burden that future generations will be forced to shoulder. The end of the Liberal Democratic Party's (LDP) more than half-century reign and the advent of the new government led by the Democratic Party of Japan (DPJ) may touch off a complete departure from the inclination toward government intervention that Japan once required.

At the end of 2008, when the Lehman shock reached Japanese shores, the Japanese government's net assets—including those of local governments and social security programs—became nearly zero. An increase in pension benefit payments in line with the aging of the population eroded the assets of social security plans, contributing to a decrease in the government's overall net assets.

Japan's working population peaked slightly after the mid-1990s. Until then, the assets of social security programs had naturally been on the upward trend. Also, the economic bubble in the second half of the 1980s enabled the government to issue no current expenditure deficit-covering bonds in 1990, as it was able to cover the current expenditure with tax revenue alone. At the end of 1991, the government's net assets reached their peak at about 350 trillion yen.

This coincided with the end of the Cold War, and it was a unique opportunity for Japan to reexamine its post–World War II methods of economic management. However, as the perception that Japan was the true winner of the Cold War prevailed even in the United States, there was no inclination to encourage attempts to reform Japan's economic approach.

In those years, however, Japan was entering a stage where it needed to fundamentally change the design of its economic system. First of all, the baby boomers were reaching their mid-forties. In spite of the fact that, in twenty years or so, they would be reaching pension age — and more than 6 million new pensioners would emerge over three years — no changes were made to the pay-as-you-go public pension system, in which the working population finances the benefits for pensioners.

Because the onset of population decline had already been predicted, Japan should have taken action to change the situation in which pensioners have to rely on the contributions to the pension program of the working generation, who in turn must depend on future generations' willingness to pay pension premiums. In short, the government should have shifted at that time to a funded pension system, although the problem of one working generation having to pay double for its own pensions as well as for pensions of the current retirees would have surfaced during the transition period.

Yet Japan left pension-system reform unaddressed. Hypothetically, the government could have set aside about 100 trillion yen of the 350 trillion yen in net assets as reserves to cushion the burden of dual payments on the working generation. The government could have issued 100 trillion yen worth of perpetual bonds, like the British consols (consolidated stocks, a type of government bond), for which the government is obliged to pay only interest, with the government's annual current expenditure used for the interest payments. Meanwhile, the 100 trillion yen could have been used to make up for a shortfall in pension assets to pay benefits to existing pensioners. If a precise calculation showed that 100 trillion yen was not enough, the government could have issued 150 trillion yen in perpetual bonds.

If these measures had been taken, it would have had a wealth effect on generations who were approaching the pension age. Also, younger generations could have avoided the feeling that the public pension program puts them at a disadvantage in terms of contributions and benefits as a result of demographic changes.

The payment of interest on perpetual bonds would have required a cut in the government expenditure on other items, or a tax increase, or both. But that would have been a one-time cost stemming from the pension changeover, and the wealth effect could have put the Japanese economy on track for balanced development.

In reality, however, the LDP government behaved like the winner of the Cold War. It appeared to think that there was nothing wrong with its past and present approach. When the growth of demand finally slowed in the wake of the collapse of the economic bubble and the Japanese economy confronted systemic risk around 1998, the government took steps in line with its winning formula—stimulus by boosting fiscal spending. They called the measures Keynesian policies. Since then, the national debt has continued to swell, with the government likely having faced a negative net worth at the end of 2009.

The government sector's balance sheet at the end of 2008, shortly before the amount of debt exceeded that of assets, showed total assets at 995 trillion yen—including nonfinancial assets, such as roads and land, of 491 trillion yen and financial assets of 504 trillion yen. With the debt coming to 984 trillion yen, net worth was 12 trillion yen. Because the net assets in 2008 were down almost 50 trillion yen from a year earlier, it seemed inevitable that the government would face negative net worth at the end of 2008.

The theory of prominent British economist Arthur Pigou that the wealth effect helps turn around the economic situation should have been appreciated in Japan twenty years ago. But back then, few in the country referred to the economic stabilization effects of the funded pension system. This underscores that arguments based on the closed economy—the premise of Keynesian thinking—have been the over-whelming mainstream in Japan, in defiance of the reality of spreading economic globalization.

In 2010, under the DPJ government, it is effectively impossible to convert to the Pigou theory. Given the negative net worth in the government balance sheet, the idea of issuing a massive amount of perpetual government bonds is simply unrealistic. In the first place, the DPJ would not focus on the wealth effect in formulating the economic policy.

In today's circumstances, whose study can Japan refer to in order to emerge from the recession? The answer is probably that of Austrian economist Joseph Schumpeter, who preached the need for innovation. Through innovation, which heightens added value and creates new customers, Japan should seek to multiply the government's net assets. Perhaps, as the first step, a renewed emphasis ought to be put on research and development.

China Flexes Muscles, Moves toward Free Markets

If any country has begun intentionally reshaping the global economic map in the wake of the Lehman shock, it would be China. Although Beijing has not announced any intention to become hegemonic, it absolutely considers the U.S.-dominated world a thing of the past.

With regard to the future of the dollar, the world's principal reserve currency, China is willing to offer a specific proposal on the international financial architecture of the future. One factor, though, continues to act as a drag on Beijing's ambitions: its own financial system remains a far cry from a free market. Without a uniform domestic market, the country has a long way to go before achieving free price formation, and the reality is that it continues to call for a harmonious society.

On March 31, 2010, China lifted a ban on six leading domestic brokerages conducting margin trades on the Shanghai and Shenzhen stock exchanges, allowing individuals to take long and short positions by borrowing funds and shares. The margin trading program is still limited; such transactions are allowed only for fifty Shanghai-listed stocks and forty Shenzhen-traded issues that are considered to have sufficient liquidity. But the move illustrates Beijing's desire to increase trading volume on the stock markets. Trading of stock index futures was introduced in April 2010 as well.

It has been three years since liquidity started drying up around the world and the financial crisis was observed to be moving forward. The crisis had been triggered by the failure of a U.S. nonbank lender that formed and sold subprime loans. Because a leading state-run bank in China was purchasing securitized products, Beijing had no choice but to clarify its policy and get involved in the global financial system. In November 2007, the Bank of China held a seminar at which it answered participants' questions. Many of the questioners wondered how much damage Chinese banks had suffered.

One of the speakers explained that the proportion of exposure to toxic assets was limited and the health of assets at state-owned banks was, in principle, not undermined. Investors appeared unsatisfied with the level of disclosure but did not press the matter.

China's economic criticism of the United States has been contradictory. The possibility that Washington's dollar payments to other countries would be denied was close to zero. So while recognizing the greenback's acceptability, the argument that the United States had been unfairly buying many valuable assets in the world with IOUs is a valid theory. However, on the other side, China has become an industrial structure reliant on such dollar dispersion.

So China began calling for an international payment mechanism that replaces the dollar as the reserve currency. It later argued that improvements should be made to the international financial system through reform of the IMF, as part of its effort to overcome the contradiction at the minimum cost possible. From 2008 through 2009, China even came up with the idea of joint research at economic institutions in China and Russia of a settlement system denominated in special drawing rights (SDRs).

China, Japan, and Russia are the three top holders of foreign currency reserves, which indicates that the three nations are the world's main collectors. Apparently Beijing came up with the idea of replacing the U.S. currency with SDRs to create a framework for a new international financial architecture. My institution, the Center for International Public Policy Studies, was asked to join the study.

My reply was no, because there was no scenario of the dollar's deposition for the following two reasons.

One is that SDRs, which are used only for IMF settlements, will never become a global currency. While the dollar can be called the reserve currency because of its high acceptability in the private sector, the lack of a solid global agreement supporting SDRs makes the chances that SDRs will be accepted by the private sector in the future almost nil.

Another reason is that in many cases, foreign currency reserves do not reflect the economic strength of a sovereign nation but rather illustrate the absence of functionality in its internal economic mechanisms or the rigidity of the system. With respect to the foreign currency reserves in China, Japan, and Russia, it can be said that such weaknesses experienced by these countries at a certain point in time directly led to their buildups of dollars. If a completely floating exchange rate regime were to be adopted, foreign reserves would come down close to zero, as seen in the case of EU member states. So foreign reserves can be said to indicate the magnitude of rigidity and have nothing to do with proving capability to reform reality.

In 2008, China began considering letting the yuan, which had been pegged to the U.S. dollar, fluctuate along a wider band. It even started reforming its stock markets.

What do all these moves mean? The collapse of Japan's economic bubble was triggered by the trading of stock index futures. Before the Nikkei stock average climbed to flirt with the 40,000 mark at the end of 1989, some foreign investors started building short futures positions. To hedge the risk of the stock market's further upturn, these investors bought the underlying instruments and witnessed share prices trending down from February to March 1990. They covered their short positions by buying assets back at lower prices and, to lock in profits, sold their holdings of the underlying stocks. All of a sudden, stock prices began spinning down.

Arguing that futures trades are influencing transactions of their underlying assets is tantamount to the tail wagging the dog, a Tokyo Stock Exchange director said. The director, who was formerly with the Finance Ministry, called on the Osaka Securities Exchange, where stock index futures are traded, for voluntary restraint. He even visited the Singapore Exchange, which was handling the products, to complain.

China is without a doubt seeking to enhance the maturity of the market by adding to the depth of the capital markets. The idea of creating a market that might replace those in New York City and London is clearly more legitimate than improving the settlement system with SDRs. As part of nurturing of a market, Beijing might have even started anticipating insurrection of the market to add discipline to its macroeconomic policy.

Still, even these enlightened people are not planning to introduce such legitimate techniques through open discussions. In other words, without debating the significance of such techniques, they have already begun the introduction procedures as if they are simply handling paperwork. Why is China working to attain reform that could drastically change the landscape of the global economy in a manner similar to the handling of paperwork?

This is because there is an opposition force within the Chinese leadership. Provinces and other regional jurisdictions around the country have established off-the-books development corporations to acquire real property. Such unrestrained development coincided with the central government's 4 trillion yuan ($585.9 billion) investment announced in 2008, leading to a bubble.

Given this situation, it is not unnatural to think that those who built up speculative long positions are linked to some leaders within the Communist Party of China. With the question of how to introduce the collapse of the bubble, the paperwork handling may actually be a product of wisdom. We may be about to see the coincidence of a shift in the global economic landscape and a change in the domestic landscape in China.

Innovate, Be Wary of Global Warming

When we look at world history in ten-year increments, we see an accelerating pace of change in which even quite drastic projections are outpaced by reality.

Snapshot of the Past Fifty Years

The first half of the 1960s was marked by economic stability. But in the second half, the U.S. military action in Vietnam led to an acceleration of inflation, darkening the global outlook.

In the 1970s, as the North vs. South conflict surfaced, the international framework for managing oil and other resources came under question. Two oil crises undermined the economic management skills of industrialized nations, and the Group of Seven was launched. Discussion agendas included not only fiscal, financial, foreign exchange, and trade policies but also strategies for addressing matters related to the Soviet Union, with the aim of maintaining the liberal regime.

The speed of change picked up substantially in the 1980s. The U.S. president at the time, Ronald Reagan, increased military spending through his Strategic Defense Initiative to thwart the Soviet regime. Together with a drastic alteration to how the United States collects taxes, this led to a constant expansion of the U.S. fiscal deficit and monetary tightening. The outcome of this situation was a combination of a strong dollar and capital account surpluses (current-account deficits). One ramification was that manufacturers in the United States began full-bore outsourcing, resulting in the so-called East Asian miracle.

At the end of the 1980s, the communist economies of the Soviet Union and Eastern Europe could not even commercially produce semi-conductors. In contrast, South Korea and the three other Asian Tigers came to hold unchallenged positions on the global economic map with their quality chip fabrication. The 1989 fall of the Berlin Wall can be said to be the result of the undulating global industrial map.

The 1990s began with the dissolution of the Soviet Union and the end of the Cold War. As the United States and Western Europe enjoyed a peace dividend, post-bubble Japan failed to stick the knife into vested interests.

Meanwhile, India, China, and Brazil, in that order, took some historical turns. It was in 1991 that India, which had been applying old, Soviet-style central planning to its economy, fell into an economic crisis. Perhaps not surprisingly, the country had thrown itself into economic turmoil akin to the old Soviet Union's. But the finance minister, Man-mohan Singh, who is now prime minister, pushed for liberalization—a move described as being as important as Nehru winning independence for the Indian people.

In 1992, under the leadership of Deng Xiaoping, Chinese economic reform and deregulation gained momentum after Deng—fearful that the West might target China following the Soviets' fall—made a dramatic policy reversal. Moves toward market economies were becoming a global trend.

Rebuilding Brazil

Then Brazil began its attempt to come out of its "lost 1980s." Under the leadership of former president Fernando Cardoso, the country confirmed its policy direction by establishing fiscal discipline—and saw trust in its currency restored. This can be seen as the beginning of the full-scale rebuilding of the Brazilian economy.

Even after Luiz Inacio Lula da Silva, one of the founding members of the Workers' Party, was elected president, Brasilia continued to pay close attention to its account balance. And as the fruits of economic growth spread to the public, intellectuals in Brazil lost their excessive wariness about the United States.

With this development, the external dominance of Latin America that had been in place since the 1960s was shunted aside by economic policies. The rise of the import-substitution industrialization developed by Raul Prebisch became a thing of the past, and Latin American countries gradually grew confident about operating market economies.

At one point in Brazil, Theotonio Dos Santos's dependency theory was the dominant concept. Under this notion, core and periphery countries exist, with internal rulers in developing countries seeking to pocket gains through their connections to the core nations. As a result, the average citizen in developing economies is subject to deprivation by both rulers in their own countries and the core nations. This concept has become history forever.

At the turn of the twenty-first century, further changes were about to be made to the global economic map. The Y2K computer software issue made clear India's strong presence in global software production. Then, as the Kashmir conflict between Pakistan and India grew serious in the wake of the September 11, 2001, attacks on the United States, and as a nuclear game of one-upmanship emerged between the two neighbors, the world's heavy dependency on India's IT processing capabilities came into the spotlight. The consensus among the international community was that India could no longer be overlooked.

Following the 1999 decision by China to join the World Trade Organization (WTO)—India's accession came in 2001—foreign direct investment in that country grew rapidly. At the same time, China started to become the world's factory. In the second half of 2003, it became clear that Chinese growth was linked to the rapid increase in demand for energy and industrial materials. It also became obvious that strong growth in demand for Brazil's iron ore, coal, and grains boosted production activity in that country and the value of its currency.

It was also around this time when the links among economies such as India, China, Brazil, and South Africa became known at the WTO negotiation table. This meant that, while industrialized nations were stuck with their agriculture protection policies, they had no choice but to reflect the voices of the emerging countries in shaping the global order.

Then came the liquidity crunch in the wake of the global financial crisis triggered by the collapse of Lehman Brothers Holdings Inc. of the United States. In terms of blocking the adverse effects of the credit squeeze, emerging countries—which had gradually enhanced their economic capabilities—ended up performing better. All along a tide had been swelling, and now there is even a Group of Twenty.

On the geopolitical landscape going forward, global warming is certain to be an important and divisive issue. Developing countries will likely be classified according to how they address greenhouse-gas emissions:

- Those such as China and India that consider emission increases unavoidable if growth is to be sustained,
- Mostly oil-producing countries that do not pay much attention to the greenhouse-gas issue in the first place,
- Island and other nations that are most susceptible to global warming.

If they are to switch to low-carbon societies, industrialized economies face a new industrial paradigm. In recovering from the financial crisis, today's world needs an economic system that enables creation of value-chain management with an eye toward that new industrial paradigm and a hand on controlling risks. In this aspect, a new map will likely be drawn depending on which countries develop a framework that induces innovation (see table 1 on pages 54 and 55).

Securitization Business Holds Key for United States; Japan Faces Increasing Debt Load

The outlook for the world economy for 2010 has gotten far brighter than what was projected around the middle of 2009. The dramatic upturn is due to (1) a successful halt to the fall in demand thanks to fiscal stimulus packages adopted by countries around the world; (2) a partial recovery in financial functions following moves by governments and central banks to purchase toxic assets, albeit temporarily; and (3) a surge in demand in China and other emerging economies that has buttressed the comeback in pockets of economic activity in industrial countries.

Going forward, potential risks abound, however. Implementation of "exit strategies," together with the onset of risk factors, would be something to be averted—an eventuality that should be carefully monitored.

The image Americans had of Barack Obama before he was elected president was one of somebody who could "unify the divided America." However, in the run-up to the midterm elections, Obama has clearly taken positions in the divisive fights on political and economic issues.

The U.S. Securities and Exchange Commission's filing of a civil lawsuit against Goldman Sachs Group, Inc., is an attempt to delve into the origination and distribution of securitized products, which have formed the basis of financial innovation in the United States for nearly a quarter century. I don't think the development is unrelated to the difficult situation in which the Obama administration finds itself. In the background is the need for a government in a sovereign state to prioritize winning a taxpayer mandate.

Creating jobs poses the first and foremost task for the management of the U.S. economy, but getting the economy out of high unemployment, of around 10 percent, should be no easy job. For as long as a quarter century, consumer spending in the United States has been underpinned by financial engineering methods posited on steady prices of housing assets. But this foundation crumbled in the wake of the financial crisis, resulting in the protracted balance-sheet adjustment of the household sector.

In a bid to reduce financial systemic risk (which means a state of a continuous cutoff of liquidity), the U.S. federal government, following the bankruptcy of the fourth-biggest investment bank, was compelled to inject capital into financial institutions. Amid such turmoil, the number one and number two investment banks turned themselves into bank holding companies to avoid bankruptcy and takeovers. Then they accepted government investment to bolster their equity capital on the one hand, while on the other they squeezed their assets even at the risk of incurring losses.

These radical measures enabled market players to predict, to a greater degree of accuracy than otherwise, where prices would bottom out for bonds, currencies, and commodities, among other financial products. When prices were judged to have sunk enough to leave little room for further downward adjustments, some players issued buy orders.

In the case of Goldman Sachs, the company earned huge profits from proprietary futures trading in the fixed income, currency, and commodity fields. In 2009 and 2010, Goldman recorded only limited amounts of earnings from its main line of investment banking, including such services as brokering of mergers and acquisitions and underwriting of securities. But the company logged hefty profits in its trading division, which directly translated into large executive compensation and touched off a major anti–Wall Street chorus among taxpayers.

Table 1. Economic and Geopolitical Landscape, 2001–2015

Time period	General characteristics	Actors	Market solutions or forbearance policies	Geopolitical landscape	Historical reference	Economic school
2001–2006	Low interest rate	Alan Greenspan	Collateralized debt obligations	Favorable economic growth in the world	Washington consensus	Market-oriented policies in the global context
	Low risk profile	Bank of Japan	Securitization of subprime loans		Great moderation	
		Large financial institutions	Originate and distribute model			
2007–2008	Fears of systemic risk	Hedge funds	Capitalization on vulnerabilities	Cash is king	Disruption of money flows	Keynesian on liquidity traps
	Disruption of credit	Central banks	Building up of liquidities		Concerns of great depression	
2008–2010	Fiscal stimulus	Sovereign states	Enlarged balance sheets of central banks	Decoupling by emerging economies	No polar system	Keynesian on fiscal stimulus
	Large deficits	Fund managers	Governance problems of sovereign states		Group of Twenty	
			Financial regulations			

(table continued on next page)

Table 1. Economic and Geopolitical Landscape, 2001–2015 (*continued*)

Time period	General characteristics	Actors	Market solutions or forbearance policies	Geopolitical landscape	Historical reference	Economic school
2010–2015	Fiscal revamp	New types of financial institutions	No to "too big to fail" (U.S.)	Global crowding out phenomenon	Kyoto protocol II	Innovation theory
			Acceptance of "too big to save" (EU)	Mergers and acquisitions in emerging economies	Reduced demand for oil	
			Fiscal reconstructions	Questions on sustainability of Chinese economic growth		
	Exit policies		"Green revolution"			

Source: Author's concept.

20/20 Hindsight

In hindsight, the possibility of such problems occurring should have been determined beforehand and necessary precautions taken before taxpayer money had been injected into major banks. What I mean here concerns the details of the contracts the U.S. government signed with the banks that were teetering on the edge of bankruptcy so that the government could make an equity investment in the banks for credit-enhancement purposes.

The government made this move because losses incurred by the nation upon the surfacing of systemic risk would be unbearable, and for this reason the move would be acceptable to the taxpayer. Also, the government injected public money into the problem banks under a set of uniform rules in the fear that any differences in the amounts of injections would have been interpreted to mean that the government was rating the creditworthiness of the banks and turning particular banks into targets for investor selling. This reason also would be convincing to the taxpayer.

The problem was the fact that banks, when they managed to avert bankruptcy thanks to the infusion of public money, liberally distributed any gains made during this process to existing shareholders and employees.

An investor who decides to acquire an interest in an entity caught in a management crisis is in effect shouldering a great risk. As such, the investor can justifiably argue that his or her investment portion should be evaluated highly in the wake of a successful rescue of the target company. If this argument has its way, the imposition of a special capital gains tax on profit that is earned during a certain period following the investment decision (five years, for example) should not be categorically termed unreasonable.

There was, however, no such agreement. That is why criticism targeted at investment banks did not go any further than criticism for their exorbitant executive compensation even after the banks survived the crisis and made large profits by taking advantage of the circumstance that had befallen them. This failed institutional design very likely became one reason for the Obama administration's demeanor of unilaterally taking advantage of taxpayer reaction. There is some possibility that historians will someday judge that Obama tried to seize on this flawed design for his own partisan purposes.

This perception is, however, entirely contrary to the intent of the so-called Volcker rule. The institutional design for preventing a repeat of the too-big-to-fail bailout experience has as its aim getting the most of capitalism's functions. In this light, it is only natural that the Volcker rule will ultimately try to address the issue of containing the executives' moral hazard. The Volcker rule thus will likely achieve its initial objectives.

The problem is that the Volcker rule will possibly exert a major influence on the level of the securitization business in the United States. Within the overall structure of the securitization business, individual finance companies formed a link on the value-creation chain and did their bit for the resolution of a major task: financing the U.S. current-account deficit. If this business fails to deliver, a substantive adjustment could occur, affecting the entire United States in such a way as to lower the level of deficit financing. In that case, it would become difficult to prevent the U.S. economy from suffering medium-term stagnation.

Risk Spilling Over

Meanwhile, risks for the EU are spilling over from particular sovereign states, such as Greece, and now the eurozone's entire governance system is in question. In the first place, Europe should have asked itself a question about whether its proposed currency union would fulfill the conditions required of an "optimal currency area," a concept proposed by Robert Mundell.

Preconditions for economic integration, such as smooth movements of labor and capital, for example, should be indispensable for having a common currency. Otherwise, differences among member countries, such as boom and recession or high and low inflation rates, are not adjusted within the regional bloc, and only the costly aspect of maintaining the same currency will come into sharp focus.

The euro's debut started as an attempt to build a superstructure in Europe—a political move aimed at eliminating the West German mark so that the collapse of the Cold War structure would not undo Europe's history of economic integration. This was a tall order that resulted in schisms in the regional bloc, so that the eurozone took a direct hit from the Lehman shock.

If the euro's value wobbles over the medium term, the EU economy will inevitably suffer stagnation. As early as a year ago, Henry Kissinger referred to signs of the EU's waning capability to engage in world affairs. A year ago, the possibility of Germany coming to the rescue of the Hungarian economy was under discussion. This was part of a body of analysis on Europe's engagement capability in wider global affairs.

Now, analysis of the EU's shaky global engagement has extended to the future of the euro.

Crying Wolf

For Japan, approximately 95 percent of the outstanding issue balance of Japanese government bonds (JGBs) is held within the country. This has helped avert an eruption of sovereign risk despite Japan's abnormally high ratio of public debt to GDP, and repeated warnings about Japan's debt sailing into dangerous waters have been spurned as crying wolf.

However, we have to say that at last the moment of truth is just around the corner. This is not to say that a powder keg is about to explode. On the contrary, Japan's banking sector, unable to find borrowers who can soak up the banks' pileup of deposits, is increasing the ratio of JGBs in the banks' portfolios. As such, the yield on the forty-year JGBs, due in 2050, stands at a mere 2.2 percent.

The current Shangri-la for JGB-issuing authorities could turn to a Paradise Lost at any time. Among the plausible turnarounds toward a JGB debacle is one when the JGB balance exceeds net financial assets of Japan's households, which now total about 1 quadrillion yen ($10.6 trillion). This scenario, too awesome to ignore, leaves only several years until it comes true.

Although it is already an internationally accepted view that the sustainability of China's economic growth is an open question, study of China's economy inevitably is connected directly to analysis of risks facing the world economy (table 2). For example, if Japan decides to adopt an austere fiscal policy, its success or failure will hinge on the sustainability of high economic growth in China and other countries in East Asia. The risk factors have become interlinked.

Postcrisis Future Murky amid Unstable Global Framework

The geopolitical conditions since the recent global financial crisis can be expressed as the emergence of a perspective questioning how divergence of a global system may be prevented.

The freeze in funding flows drastically slowed economic activity. In a bid to forestall a sharp rise in unemployment, governments around the world rolled out stimulus programs at the cost of widening their fiscal deficits. This led to the creation of a temporary lull in the chaos,

Table 2. Current Risk Factors for Selected Countries and Areas

Country	Risk factors going forward	Political background	Symptomatic phenomena
United States	Inflexibility of deficit finance	Discrepancies between (1) Main Street and Wall Street and (2) Democrats and Republicans	Thin market for securitized products
			Higher long-term interest rate
European Union	Contagion of sovereign risk	Undue burdens of big sovereign states and euphoria in some parts of eurozone	Weaker euro
			Higher coupon rate for debt refinancing
Japan	Failure of rebalancing government sectors	Euphoria under Cold War regime and huge vested interest groups under Liberal Democratic Party governments	From "cry wolf" to reality as to higher rate for Japanese government bonds
			Investors' short positions on yen currencies
China	Increased inefficiencies of input-output ratio and concentration of bad assets to state-run financial institutions	Decentralized but non-market-oriented investment mechanism and distorted allocation of resources	Inflexible value of renminbi
			High dependence on imports of energy and natural resources

Source: Author's concept.

making it seem as if the "crisis of the century" had been prevented. But it also ignited the issue of sovereign risk. Greece's fiscal crisis is merely the first instance of a possible divergence of the system. Let us analyze this situation with a hexagon.

The geopolitics during the Cold War can be expressed as two pentagons. The two extremes of the United States and the former Soviet Union, through the control lines extending in four directions, prevented inconsistencies within their camps from surfacing. With respect to the

Soviet Union, it built a military mechanism through the Warsaw Pact and sought to manage nuclear weapons within countries subscribing to the treaty. When China under the leadership of Mao Zedong withdrew from such restrictions, Deng Xiaoping faced off with Mikhail Suslov in Moscow. Chinese nuclear physicists who had been dispatched to the Soviet Union returned home within days.

In Eastern Europe, no peaceful separation was possible. As shown by the Hungarian Revolution of 1956 and Prague Spring in 1968, the lines extending in all directions created a control system on the back of the dominant militaristic competence.

The control system the United States adopted was achieved in the form of Washington's forward deployment. On the Atlantic side, where a stable NATO framework was in place, the tensions existed only in the form of the Cold War, without actual battles; but in the Asia-Pacific, hot wars erupted. On the Korean Peninsula, the U.S. military established a full-fledged presence to control military expansion by the North. As China joined the conflict against the United States, which had moved to the border, the United States was forced to accept maintenance of conflict status through a cease-fire. While the competence of the U.S. military and its ideology of fighting to protect freedom were never in doubt, the sense of discomfort with communism in Asia remained, and the image of "a war that could not be won" was created.

The conflict between the United States and the Soviet Union eventually formed a situation in which the two extremes mutually relied on dominance. In their nuclear strategies, the principle of mutual assured destruction (MAD) was born. The fact that NATO had no choice but to stay on the sidelines when the Soviet military invaded Prague shows that the doctrine of MAD had spread not only among military leaders but among political leaders as well. In that sense, in terms of arresting the emergence of contradictions within their own camps, one might say that the United States and the Soviets were pursuing joint rule.

When this landscape became a thing of the past with the end of the Cold War, the two pentagons were destroyed with the start of an era in which stability is guaranteed only through system superiority. Debuting at this time was democracy in the political realm and capitalism in the economic. It was soon recognized that the entities responsible for bringing democracy and capitalism to regions that were not yet familiar with such concepts were the World Bank and the IMF, both of which are based in Washington, D.C. Such consensus out of Washington was not necessarily built on the back of military competence. For this reason, if the basic systems of collective decision making through parliaments and efficient resource allocation through markets begin to weaken, it would undermine the security framework at a fundamental level.

While European countries were forced to spend more than they wished to fight Greece's fiscal crisis, the problem of "pollution" immediately spread to the eurozone. In other words, the EU now faces the ultimate question of whether to scale back the common-currency area by separating some member states from the eurozone and providing the option of devaluing currencies, or pursuing a "federal Europe" that would perform the functions of a sovereign nation suited to the common-currency zone. Unless this question is answered, the EU's power to engage in non-European matters will not be restored.

Confidence within the United States in its system has been drastically shaken as well. The country had boasted of large numbers engaged in financial services. Its system for value creation through financial activity was supposed to symbolize the competence of the U.S. economy as well. The U.S. current-account deficit has been addressed by building financial activity of securitization into supply chain management. However, that overall structure is on the verge of collapsing. Now that competence is lost, the future of U.S. engagement in global matters has become uncertain.

In the hexagon chart (figure 1), Japan and China are presented as key players in addition to the EU and the United States. Without structural reform in Japan or China, creating an open structure of engagement in the international community would be difficult. Also shown on the chart are two anticipated outcomes. On the Atlantic side and in East Asia, no player will likely be able to display capabilities to form order through a policy of active engagement.

One GDP ranking estimate for the time around 2030 lists China, the United States, Brazil, India, and Japan as the top five countries. For such geopolitical change to be created in a stable manner, engagement capabilities on the global level must be maintained somewhere. After the two pentagons were destroyed, an unstable hexagon was established and exists today. But predicting what the future holds has become extremely difficult.

Figure 1. Instability of Global Framework: Weak Posture for Global
Engagement

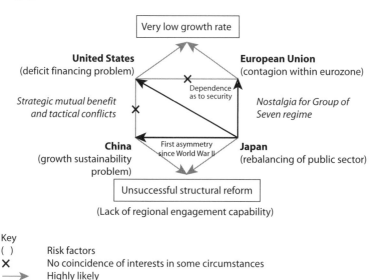

Key
( )   Risk factors
✕   No coincidence of interests in some circumstances
→   Highly likely
➤   Sympathetic approach by Japan

Germany Abandons Duality of Democracy and Market

Democracy and the market economy have long been considered insepa-
rable. Both are decentralized and based on decisions by individuals.
They also have a segmented governance structure like the stem of a
plant separated by joints.

Because of their structural similarities, democratic decision making
and the price discovery function of the market are considered to have
duality. But German chancellor Angela Merkel drove a wedge between
them with the May 18, 2010, announcement that Germany will ban
naked short selling of eurozone government bonds.

Democracy and the market economy also serve as pillars of
globalization. They have virtually become ideologies and criteria to
measure reality. The IMF and the World Bank prescribe economic as-
sistance plans based on these criteria. Their policy advice is called the
Washington consensus, named after the city where the organizations
are headquartered. Because of its link with both democracy and the
market economy, the Washington consensus has a connotation of self-

fulfilling prophecy. The prospect that China will adopt a multiparty system sometime in the future bears down on the leaders of the Chinese Communist Party because denying duality of the two principles is difficult even for communists.

Returning to Merkel, she announced the ban on naked short selling of bonds and some German financial shares without consulting other EU leaders. Some analysts said the move generated arbitrage among institutions and created fears about distorted distribution of resources as well as a lack of coordination among the eurozone members, triggering sell-offs on various financial markets. But the stock decline that began on May 18 is attributed to a partial loss of market functions. The proposed government restrictions on financial trade undermined the market's price discovery and hedging functions. Merkel must have been advised on this point by her policy advisers. She apparently chose to heed the wishes of German voters.

Her economic policy advisers must have told her the following five points: (1) A ban on naked short selling is likely to deprive investors of the means to hedge risks and lead them to refrain from making risky investments; (2) when investors do not take risks, transaction volumes will fall and the market maker system could become less efficient; (3) investors are likely to miss the opportunities to sell and buy financial products in such a situation, and they may decide to close out their positions; (4) eurozone government bonds and leading German financial issues to be covered by the ban are serving as benchmarks; if their prices are distorted by the regulation, prices of other financial products would be distorted even more; (5) if all these concerns become a reality, future generations will conclude that Greece triggered the eurozone crisis, but it was Germany that aggravated the situation.

Despite opposition to market restrictions, Merkel decided to impose the ban to side with public opinion: that speculative trading has gone too far. Why did Germany reject decentralization and segmentation of the two principles?

After suspicions about the overall amount of Greek debt emerged, German taxpayers became less tolerant of Greece, making it harder for Merkel to address the issue after the start of 2010. The EU and IMF finally agreed on a rescue package for Greece on May 10. But EU leaders should have discussed the fundamentals of Greece's economic and fiscal management, not the emergency loans. Some members of the German parliament want to oblige Greece to return to balanced finance—cutting its budget deficit to less than 0.5 percent of its gross domestic product by 2015, for instance—in the midterm. This resolute intolerance indicates that parliament is focusing on reflecting voters' will. And the chancellor can no longer ignore it.

But Germany cannot interfere with Greece's domestic affairs. All it can do is create a new standard in its own market. The ban on naked short selling shows that the government will not overlook investors who exploit fiscal vulnerabilities of sovereign states and make profits on futures markets. The ban is both a warning to speculative investors and a display of intolerance to Greece and other debt-ridden eurozone countries that are now called the "periphery." A sovereign state, along with the market, can now shake indebted countries.

The tough stance, however, has increased concerns about the single European currency. The euro's rapid decline is affecting exporters in the United States, Japan, and China. The United States cannot expect exports to lead an economic recovery. The yuan had no way but to appreciate against the dollar, and it will soar against the euro. This is an adverse wind for Chinese exporters. It has become difficult for Japanese companies to gain profits from their exports to the EU.

Sovereign risks that initially became apparent in Greece are now affecting the foundation of the global economy. German people may be feeling puzzled to see that their government's decision is drawing excessive attention. This asymmetric reaction suggests that major countries still play an important role, even in this globalization era.